THE DEAD MAN'S GUIDE TO ESTATE PLANNING

An Attorney's Field Manual For Protecting Your Family

Patrick Nolan

Chariton Media

ISBN-13: 978-1-972155-00-4

Cover design by: Patrick Nolan
Printed in the United States of America

Other Books By The Author

An Unfinished Republic:
The Architects, Warriors, and Witnesses of the Revolution

Small Claims Court Handbook:
How to Win in Any State

For my family whose many plans I missed during long late hours at work. I thank you for your patience and shall endevour to be worthy of your grace.

Estate Planning isn't gallows thinking, it is an act of love.

CONTENTS

INTRODUCTION: ESTATE PLANNING PRINCIPLES THAT CROSS STATE LINES

This book comes from my practice as an estate planning attorney in Missouri. Every example, every case study, every procedural detail reflects Missouri law as I've applied it for hundreds of families.

But here's what I've learned: the questions families ask are the same everywhere.

"What happens to my kids if I die?"

"How do I keep my ex-spouse from getting my child's inheritance?"

"Will the nursing home take everything I've built?"

"What documents does my college freshman need?"

The answers follow the same principles whether you're in Missouri, Montana, or Massachusetts. The tools might have different names—what we call a Transfer on Death Deed in Missouri might be called a Beneficiary Deed in Colorado—but the strategy is identical.

HOW TO USE THIS BOOK IF YOU LIVE OUTSIDE MISSOURI

Read for the concepts, not the specifics.

When I mention a Missouri statute or form, understand it as "ask your attorney about the equivalent in your state." Use the questions I raise as a conversation guide with your local attorney.

Most states have parallel solutions—if Missouri allows it, there's probably a version where you live.

HOW TO USE THIS BOOK IF YOU LIVE IN MISSOURI

Everything in here applies directly to you. The laws, forms, procedures, and time frames are current as of February 2026.

That said, estate planning is highly individual—this book educates you on what's possible, but you still need an attorney to implement a plan tailored to your situation.

I'm a veteran of the 3rd Armored Cavalry Regiment and a former reporter. Both careers taught me the same lesson: a good plan executed today beats a perfect plan that never happens.

This book won't make you an estate planning expert. But it will make you an informed client who asks better questions and makes faster decisions.

Let's get started.

SECTION 1: WHY ESTATE PLANNING MATTERS

ESTATE PLANNING MYTHS THAT TRIP UP YOUNG ADULTS

The False Beliefs That Leave People Unprepared

I've heard it at kitchen tables and across plastic waiting room chairs—young adults itelling themselves estate planning only matters for the rich, the old, or those settled with families. They say, "I don't own anything, so why plan?" That idea is common. It delays people from handling paperwork and conversations that matter most when life turns. It's an excuse, but it's also a misunderstanding. The guts of estate planning—naming who decides for you, protecting your basic property, giving guidance—protect anyone, at any age. Failing to set something up early can leave those closest to you scrambling if there's a wreck or a bad night in the ER.

Put simply, most people don't know what estate planning really covers. It's not just about handing out money. It's about clear instructions for the storm no one sees coming.
Every state has its own rules. Even if your net worth looks like a sad number, planning now means less mess if things go wrong. It covers what happens in probate, who speaks for you, and what happens to things—digital or real—that matter more than you think.

Busting the Myths That Hold Young Adults Back

Myth #1: *"I Don't Have Enough for a Will or Trust"*

Some say, "I rent. I owe more than I have. No reason for a will." That misses the point. Most young adults, even broke ones, still have something—maybe a checking account, keepsakes, a used car, or just passwords for photos and social media. If you die, state law (not you) decides where it all goes. Intestacy is a cold process. Your wishes or gut instincts get left out.

A basic will—just a few pages—lets you appoint someone you trust to wrap up your affairs. Maybe a parent. Maybe a friend. It keeps loved ones from slogging through a long, expensive probate court mess. Without it, someone else decides, and property can land in the wrong hands. People also forget things like beneficiary designations. Retirements, insurance policies, bank accounts—these need names. If you do nothing, they default in ways you probably wouldn't pick.

Myth #2: *"Only for Parents, Married Couples, or People with Dependents"*

No spouse or kids? Doesn't get you off the hook. Die without a will, and the intestate chart sends your property up a family tree: parents, then siblings, then out to the fringes. Friends, partners, or charities you cared about? Left out. You also lose the chance to pick who handles your business when you're gone. The state assigns someone or leaves the family to fight it out.

More critical is what happens if you're alive but can't speak up. Powers of attorney and healthcare directives—these pick who decides for you about money or medical treatment. Without them, families often have to haul everyone to court, trying to get legal standing for what you would have wanted. It costs. It wears people down. And it's preventable.

Myth #3: *"I'm Too Young to Worry About Incapacity or End-of-Life"*

You can be healthy at breakfast and on a ventilator by dinnertime. Accidents don't care about youth. Having durable powers of attorney for finances and healthcare lets you choose. Otherwise, a judge may hand control to an estranged cousin or a third party who doesn't know you at all.

Turn 18, and your parents can't call the hospital to check on you, nor do your banking if you're laid up. HIPAA and privacy laws make a wall. A few sheets of paper—health care proxy, HIPAA release—patch the wall. Without them, emergencies become gridlock, and the simplest tasks get tangled.

Myth #4: *"Estate Planning Is Complicated and Costs a Fortune"*

Lawyers joke about thick binders and billable hours, but most young adults don't need that.
Most state's laws support streamlined, affordable documents if you know which ones matter. Many attorneys offer sensible packages for young people, not expensive trusts made for millionaires. You don't have to spend a pile to get it right.

Downloadable templates, though tempting, are risky. State signature rules or witness requirements are strict. Get one thing wrong, and your plan vanishes when it's needed most. An attorney's guidance now—just for the basics—can avert big messes and bigger expenses down the road.

Myth #5: *"If I Die, My Student Loans Fall on My Family"*

Student loans are no small worry. Federal loans? They die with you. But private loans, not always. Some carry claims to cosigners, or estates. Your parents could get calls if the paperwork wasn't clear, especially with smaller banks or lenders that like to fish in probate claims.

Know your debt—what rules apply to it, what benefits it has, how it plays out if you're gone. Spell it out for whoever's handling your estate. It can save grieving families from nasty surprises just as they're trying to process loss.

Steps Young Adults Should Take Right Now:

Start with Key Documents—Don't Wait. No matter your age

or net worth, every responsible person should have these on file:

- **Last Will and Testament:**
  States who gets what, and who's in charge.
- **Durable Power of Attorney for Finances:**
  Lets someone pay your bills and handle accounts if you can't.
- **Durable Power of Attorney for Health Care:**
- Names who will make medical decisions and carry out your wishes.
- **Living Will (Advance Directive):**
  Lays out what you want at the end of life, especially life support.
- **HIPAA Authorization:**
  Grants access to medical records for those you trust in an emergency.

Don't skip beneficiary designations. Bank forms, retirement paperwork, and life insurance—fill in who you want. Your state's pay-on-death and transfer-on-death options keep more out of court and in the right hands.

Don't Ignore Your Digital World

A lot of value today sits on a phone or laptop—crypto, email, even photo archives. Most old-school wills ignore this. Most states let you name a digital executor. You can specify access instructions or logins through a digital asset memo attached to your will. Without one, accounts can get locked up for good, and important memories may vanish. Write it down. Be clear. Make it easy for someone to settle up without a fight with tech companies.

Cover Pets, Cars, and Keepsakes

It sounds small—who gets your dog, or your first guitar, or the car with your stickers on it—but families can fall out over things like this. State law helps: you can specify pet care or use a TOD for cars with the Department of Revenue. If you care about what happens, spell it out and leave nothing to chance or courtroom arguments.

Update Regularly—Life Changes, So Should Your Plan

Early adulthood is chaos. New bank accounts, new cities, new people in your circle. Your plan from five years ago may be outdated already. State law can change, too. Check in with your attorney whenever your life takes a turn. Make sure the pages still fit your reality.

Clearing the Fog: What You Gain When You Plan Ahead

A few basic documents, done early, clear the road for everyone you care about. You get a say in what matters. You spare your family from red tape, confusion, and maybe from each other's tempers. It's not hard, not expensive, and every step moves you from guesswork to certainty.

Myths hold people back until life's worst moments force action. Brush them aside. Do the work up front. When you do, your wishes stand, your loved ones have clear instructions, and you get to walk through adulthood knowing you're covered—whatever comes next.

ESTATE PLANNING: AN ACT OF LOVE

Paperwork Is Secondary—It's About the People Left Behind

A man sits at his kitchen table late at night, papers spread out—wills, powers of attorney, maybe a trust draft with coffee ring stains. Military veterans know this feeling: the subtle weight of responsibility for others. Planning for death is hard to face. The forms get all the attention, but the drive is always the same—making sure the people you love aren't left adrift.

Estate planning is more than carving up assets or chasing tax savings. You do this work now so your family won't have to sort it out after you're gone. You take the punches up front. The real benefit is hidden: you keep the load off your family's shoulders when their guard is down. It's not paperwork. It's patching the roof before the storm hits, not after.

Those who ignore planning fall under the state's default rules. The courts call it intestacy, and probate marches forward, ticking off boxes without caring who gets hurt. The system takes charge—assets go on a conveyor belt, relationships and family history aside. Probate drags, legal bills stack up, fights break out over small things. The planning you do now spares your loved ones from courthouse benches and family rifts. People need room to mourn, not bureaucratic headaches.

Real Protection Takes Foresight, Not Luck

When you build an estate plan, you're telling your family:

"I won't leave you guessing." It's blunt. It's clear. Real clarity is a kind of mercy. Without a plan, your family is left searching the house for clues to your wishes. With a plan, they know where they stand.

Less Chaos When Grief Comes

Death drops in, and life gets chaotic. Nobody calls lawyers unless they have to. But if you left no clear roadmap, your family is stuck sorting through your intentions with grief pressing down. It can get messy: arguments, hard feelings, sometimes even lawsuits over trinkets you thought had no value at all.

A plan—covering the house in Kansas City, a shop in Springfield, an old truck on blocks in the Ozarks—gives your family direction. A valid power of attorney means someone you trust can step in if illness strikes. Healthcare directives prevent your loved ones from agonizing over medical choices. These documents aren't just about property; they spare your family from making the impossible call when you can't speak for yourself.

Shielding Those Who Need It Most

Estate planning lets you step in for your weakest link even after you're gone. If you've got
young kids, you can pick the right guardian instead of letting a judge do it blind. For a family member with a disability, a special needs trust keeps their care intact without risking state aid.

You can drip assets out for a young heir, not drop a lump sum in their lap. That's called teaching caution—hard-earned and often overlooked. In second marriages or blended families, a careful plan means no one winds up excluded or surprised. The system by default doesn't care about step-children or family grievances; you have to write that story yourself.

Keeping the House Together, Keeping the Family Intact

If you want the home, business, or heirlooms to stay in the family, the law gives you tools. A living trust, a beneficiary deed, a well-built will—each can keep your assets out of probate court. Without these, creditors and lawyers can eat up generations of work.

But the bigger threat is usually family conflict. Clear documents, signed and witnessed, defuse tension before it has a chance to destroy the family table. Hard truths spoken in writing can keep old wounds from reopening. If you want certain items to go to certain people, say it now. Don't make your kids fight over it later.

Legacy Isn't Just Dollars—It's What You Stand For

Every farm, business, or passing of the family cabin carries more than a price tag. These choices define who carries on your work after you're gone. Estate planning delivers not just cash, but principles.

Making Your Values Clear

A will or trust does more than cut checks. It's a statement —this mattered, this didn't. Through your plan, you can support your local church in St. Louis, a Columbia animal shelter, or seed a scholarship fund. Gifts outlast handshakes. They build traditions.

Farms and shops get split or lost when you don't spell out your wishes. It's easy to toss words around in life; it's harder to set out who should run the place and who should simply inherit. With clear instructions, one child keeps the farm running. Others share in a way that fits. Same for small businesses: leadership stays steady when you point to the next in line. Without that call, the whole operation can fall apart.

Teaching by Example—One Last Time

Passing on cash is easy. Passing on steady judgment is harder. Letters of intent, notes in your own hand, even a recording tucked in the safe—they turn dry instructions into something personal. Your reasons show through. People need to know not just what you did, but why. That carries weight when you're not there to answer follow-up questions.

Sometimes, sudden money ruins a life. If beneficiaries aren't ready, use a trust or set an age for them to inherit. Place someone steady as trustee, to guide them just long enough. That's not controlling from the grave; it's giving them a fighting chance.

How to Start Protecting the People You Love

Getting your plan together isn't a mountain. It just means looking straight at what you own and who needs protection, then doing the next sensible thing.

Here's the direct route for families:

- List your property—houses, land, old IRA, family photos or a side business out on Route 66.
- Pick someone you trust to act for you if you can't—whether that's as power of attorney or executor.
- Think about weak spots: a child with special needs, an ex-spouse still stirring trouble, kids who don't get along.
- Check your life insurance and retirement account beneficiaries. Make sure the paperwork matches your plan.
- Use a lawyer who knows local rules. Laws change, families shift.
  Keep your plan alive, don't leave it in a drawer gathering dust.

Tell your family the hard truths now. Let them know what role they'll play, and why.
The law lets you put down almost any arrangement you'd want —if you bother to spell it out while you still can.

Life changes—marriage, divorce, a new grandchild, losing your job. That's when you update your plan. Showing up for this work again and again is its own quiet form of love, even if nobody but you knows it at the time.

No One Plans for Uncertainty—You Plan for People

You can leave behind two things: a mess or a map. Every line in your will or trust is a clear decision that shields your family from the worst sort of guessing. It's grounded kindness—real, not sentimental. You show up for your people one last time, in a way that outlives you.

In every town, from farmhouse gate to city walk-up, it's the same. Make your plan. Spare them the courtroom. Leave them with your voice, not just your possessions. That's how you make the hard road gentler for the ones coming after.

SECTION 2: CORE DOCUMENTS

WHY A TRUST FOR YOUR CHILD SHOULD MATURE WITH YOUR CHILD

From the moment a child is born, a parent feels an instinctive drive to protect and nurture. We childproof our homes, carefully choose schools, offer guidance through adolescence, support their careers, and watch with pride as they start their own lives.

The desire to be there for them extends beyond emotional and physical care. Finances also play a crucial role, and without proper planning, even the best intentions—yours or theirs—can fall short.

With the future in mind, you may have established a trust for your child at birth or shortly after, knowing that you would not always be there to financially support them. However, just as children outgrow toys, clothes, and bedtime stories, they can also outgrow the terms of the inheritance you created for them in their early life. A trust that worked when your child was 5 years old may no longer meet their needs and protect them effectively at 25, 35, or 45.

Like your living, breathing child, the trust you create for them must grow as they do. It should be a flexible, evolving legal tool that matures alongside them, from first steps to first jobs, from childhood to adulthood. You may not always be there, but with the right trust setup and thoughtful updates, your care and protection can be.

Trusts for Minors

Parents look at their newborns and think they are perfect just the way they are. Nothing needs changing. But as the years pass, can you say the same about the estate plan you made long ago for their benefit?

If a minor inherits money and property outright—whether through a will or
beneficiary designation on an account such as a 401(k) or life insurance policy—they generally cannot access those funds until they reach the age of majority (age 18 in most states). While they are minors, managing and using any money and property given to them will likely require court involvement. And that process is rarely as picture-perfect as the child it is meant to protect.

Here is what happens if a minor inherits without a trust in place:

A court typically appoints a guardian of the estate (called a conservator in some states) to manage the funds. That person may not be someone you would have chosen yourself, and they must operate under strict judicial oversight.

The guardian of the estate is required to act in the child's best interest, but their actions are limited by court-ordered spending restrictions, public reporting, and annual accounting. Also, what the guardian and the court consider to be in your child's best interest may not align with what you believe is best for them. Without clear instructions in a legal document, the guardian of the estate may have no way of knowing your true intentions.

When the child reaches age 18 or 21, depending on the state, the entire balance of the account that was managed with court oversight is then handed over to them with no further guidance or restrictions—ready or not.

Conservatorship (or guardianship) is an impersonal, inflexible process. Worse, it means losing control over who manages your child's inheritance, how it is used, and when your child receives it.

A trust bypasses this system entirely and allows you to do the following:

- Appoint someone you trust (such as a family member, professional, or corporate trustee) to manage your child's inheritance.
- Specify how the money can be used and for what, such as education, healthcare, living expenses, enrichment, other essentials, or at the trustee's complete discretion
- Delay your child's full access to their inheritance beyond age 18 or 21 using staggered distributions, trustee discretion, or milestones such as completing college or reaching financial literacy goals. Learn more about naming a guardian for your minor children.

A trust lets you protect your child's future on your terms. You know your children best—and you know that they may not be ready to manage an inheritance just because the calendar says that they are 18. By using a trust and appointing someone who is responsible for managing their money for them while they are still coming of age, you can set your child up with an inheritance structure that is (almost) as perfect as they are.

Trusts for Young Adults

Your child will not remain a child forever. Part of being a parent is accepting their transition from childhood to adulthood. However, that does not always mean letting go of the reins all at once.

The idea that a child will magically become financially responsible at a fixed age such as 18, 21, or even 25 is often unrealistic. Most young adults are still in school or just beginning their careers in their early 20s. They may be juggling student loans, entry-level jobs, or their first serious relationship.

This stage of life is about experimentation and exploration. As you likely remember, early adulthood is not a straight line. It is full of detours, resets, and reimagined goals. A sudden inheritance during this phase may be overwhelming and could derail hard-earned progress.

Most young adults lack experience with budgeting, investing, and identifying financial red flags, whether they come in the form of peer pressure, risky ventures, or scams. A windfall might unintentionally discourage long-term planning, education, or steady employment. A thoughtfully designed trust can ease your children into financial responsibility and help them avoid rough spots on the road to adulthood.

Trusts can be structured with age-based distributions (e.g., 25 percent at age 21, another portion at age 25, and the rest at a later age), or they can give the successor trustee full discretion to decide when your child is ready to receive part or all of their inheritance.

Trusts can also structure inheritance distributions to encourage certain behaviors—such as staying gainfully employed by matching distributions to earned income—or reward certain achievements—such as providing a lump-sum gift upon college graduation.

These options allow you to slowly release the trust's reins, giving your child time to grow, mature, and take control when the road is not so bumpy and the path ahead is clearer.

At the same time, not all young adults mature at the same pace or share the same goals. Some are precocious, others are late bloomers. Some may be ready to handle money responsibly in their late teens or early 20s, while others need guidance well into their 30s. They may want to start a business, travel, become an artist, enter public service, or experiment with investing.

A flexible trust makes allowances for child-specific differences in personalities and goals. It can encourage financial maturity by paying for or providing distributions of the child's inheritance if they complete personal finance courses or work with a financial advisor or other type of mentor who can help them responsibly manage their funds.

It can transition from having a third-party trustee to allowing the child to act as a co-trustee or even sole trustee once they demonstrate readiness. It allows the trustmaker to create different trust structures for each of their children, taking into account their individual life paths and maturity levels.

Letting your child gradually take on financial responsibility within the protective frame of a trust prepares them for full independence. They can learn, safely make mistakes, and grow into a confident steward of their inheritance.

Trusts for Changing Needs and Grown-Up Responsibilities

Not only do children change as they grow up but the circumstances around them are also continually shifting. A trust must be malleable enough to conform to their evolving needs, emerging risks, and new family roles as your child matures into full adulthood.

Teenagers and young adults often require support for college, vocational training, or career startup costs. As adults, they may need help with major purchases, such as a home, or with long-term goals, like retirement planning.

But what about financial needs that we do not see coming? A trust must
prepare for the unexpected every bit as much as the expected.

Establishing a career is rarely straightforward. A change in jobs or career path, the decision to go back to school, a business venture, or an investment opportunity might necessitate access to funds in ways not originally conceived.

Not every adult becomes a prudent money manager. Addiction, reckless spending, manipulative relationships, or a propensity to fall for get-rich-quick schemes are a few reasons why some beneficiaries might need more guardrails. A spendthrift clause can help protect the trust's accounts and property from a child's bad decisions, creditors, and other financial risks.

Estate planning for your child involves contemplating the unthinkable: What if something happens to you? It should also ask an arguably more difficult question: What if something happens to them? An accident or disability can strike your child at any time. If they find themselves requiring needs-based government benefits (e.g., Medicaid or Supplemental Security Income), a properly structured trust can preserve access to benefits while continuing to support their quality of life.

Marriage is a major life event, but so is divorce—the statistics on failed marriages are sobering. An outright inheritance may become marital property (and possibly subject to division in a divorce) if your child commingles the funds or property with their spouse. Holding your child's inheritance in a trust can help ensure that what you leave them remains separate and protected—and solely with your child.

If your child becomes a parent, their financial picture and priorities will likely shift. You may need to amend your trust to reflect that change, whether by allowing distributions to support your grandchildren's education or by changing the trust to support a long-term, multigenerational wealth strategy.

Large estates in particular might realize tax benefits from dynasty trusts, which are designed to grow over time and provide for multiple generations, including grandchildren and great-grandchildren, for many years or even decades to come.

A Trust That Grows Up with Your Child

Sometimes being too strict with your children can backfire. The same is true of a trust: One that is too rigid may not hold up to real-life pressures and forces. Here are a few steps essential to creating and maintaining a flexible trust that can bend but not break:

- Schedule regular reviews.
  Revisit the trust every three to five years or after major life events such as graduation, marriage, divorce, an adverse health diagnosis, or the birth of a grandchild.
- Choose the righttrustee (and backup). Choose a successor trustee who understands your family values and your child's unique needs. As your child matures, consider whether they are ready to serve as successor co-trustee with the person you selected or as successor trustee on their own.
- Educate your child along the way.
  As your child matures, engage them in conversations about the trust's purpose and mechanics to build financial literacy and ease the transition of responsibility.
- Design with adaptability in mind.
  Life rarely follows a script. Incorporate discretionary authority, milestone-based provisions, or amendment language so that the trust can adapt when life takes an unexpected turn.
- Work with the right professionals.
- An estate planning attorney may be able to update trust provisions to align them with your child's path, wherever it takes them, and revise the trust to reflect current law, tax rules, government benefits eligibility, and wider economic circumstances depending on when the changes need to be made.

No amount of planning can anticipate everything that life might throw our way. Life does not remain static, and neither should the trust you create for your child. Circumstances change, people change, and a trust must also change to keep pace.

IRREVOCABLE TRUSTS: REAL-WORLD GUIDE

Irrevocable Trusts—What They Are and What They Aren't

Handing over control doesn't come easy. With an irrevocable trust, that's exactly what you do. You take assets—land, savings, insurance, whatever carries your name—and formally transfer them into a separate legal shell. From that point, you don't get to reach back in. You don't amend or revoke at will. This transfer is permanent unless the beneficiaries all sign off on a change.

There's nothing casual about the process. Where a revocable trust leaves you with an escape route—a road back if you want it—an irrevocable trust locks the door behind you. At first glance, that kind of finality can feel harsh. You lose direct power. But for many, especially those looking to shield assets, reduce tax drag, or qualify for public programs later in life, that permanence is the very tool they need.

Seeing the Practical Side: Why Some Trusts Don't Bend

Irrevocable trusts aren't academic. They're defensive maneuvers, sometimes a shield, sometimes a map for what comes after you're gone. Their advantages depend on your situation—age, profession, what you own, and who might want a piece of it.

Protecting What You've Built

Everyone watching the news knows lawsuits and creditors never sleep. Assets moved into an irrevocable trust step outside your personal risk. If you're a doctor with malpractice worries, a business owner, even just cautious about old debts, this separation can stop future claimants cold—at least if you set it up before the trouble starts. Try to sidestep creditors after the fact, though, and courts can break the trust wide open.

Navigating Medicaid and Long-Term Care

Aging brings its own calculations. Nursing homes drain life savings fast, and Medicaid comes with strict asset scrutiny. Most states follows the federal five-year "look-back" period, counting any assets you've given away or shifted into trusts in that window. Those who plan ahead—often years in advance—can move certain family assets into an irrevocable trust, protecting them and still qualifying for aid when the time comes. Misstep on the timing, though, and you're penalized, sometimes left waiting for coverage that won't come.

Trimming Estate Taxes

Many states don't hit estates with a state-level death tax anymore. The IRS still has its say on larger fortunes. The right irrevocable trust strips assets out of your taxable estate—life insurance trusts are the classic move—keeping more money with your heirs and less with the government when that final calculation shows up.

Writing the Story of Your Legacy

Not all heirs are ready for a windfall. Some folks use irrevocable trusts to stagger an inheritance—release funds after college, on birthdays, or when a child hits a set age. Others fence assets off from ex-spouses, creditors, even from the heirs themselves if poor decisions are likely. The trust's limits carry forward your intentions, past your own reach.

The Building Blocks: Roles and Rules Inside Trusts

A trust is just paper until the people involved set it in motion. The lines are drawn pretty clearly.

- The Grantor
- This is the one calling the shots at the start—usually someone of sound mind, the bar set much like for writing a will. The grantor names beneficiaries, picks a trustee, spells out who gets what and when. Once they sign and transfer assets, their power dries up fast.
- The Trustee
- Trustees carry the weight. The law calls it a fiduciary duty—care, loyalty, and impartiality. That means acting for the beneficiaries, not themselves. Sometimes it's a family member or close friend. Other times it's a bank, lawyer, or trust company. Pick someone who will keep clear records, stay organized, and avoid drama. A careless trustee ruins the whole thing.
- The Beneficiaries
- Every trust points toward someone—usually a person, sometimes an organization. The original document lays out how assets are divided, under what rules, and in what order. Trusts can even hand beneficiaries the power to approve changes or shut things down early if the situation warrants.

The Document: Where It All Gets Real

Every step, every safeguard, sits in the trust document itself. The best trusts set clear rules for the trustee, describe exactly when and how to cut checks or transfer property, and lay out how reporting and final handoffs work when the trust finally ends.

Most Common Irrevocable Trust Types

No two families build their legacies the same way. State laws give some flexibility in design, but a few trust forms pop up over and over.

Irrevocable Life Insurance Trust (ILIT)

Life insurance proceeds can become a tax drag for big estates, unless you plan ahead. An ILIT takes the policy out of your personal estate. The trust owns and pays for the policy. When it pays out, the money lands in the trust—not your taxable pile. Terms control when beneficiaries get their share.

Special Needs Trust

Families with a disabled child or adult lean on special needs trusts. These carve out money for extras—without crossing lines that would disqualify the beneficiary from Medicaid or SSI. The trust holds the assets under strict rules, sometimes for life.

Charitable Trusts

Philanthropy has its own routes. Charitable trusts let people earmark funds for good causes, often earning a tax benefit for themselves and reducing the estate size at death. Some flow during the donor's life, others start after.

Medicaid Asset Protection Trust

For families where nursing home bills are looming, this form holds assets outside countable Medicaid resources—again, if set up early and tightly. Getting it wrong can mean lost eligibility and even clawbacks from the state.

The Steps: *Making an Irrevocable Trust*

This isn't something you whip up with a handshake. No statute says you must hire an attorney, but skip legal help and you roll the dice, since a botched trust can hurt more than it helps.

Drafting the Paperwork

Start with a clear document. Name your grantor, trustee,

and beneficiaries. Spell out the trust's intent and what assets it holds. Specify how and when distributions happen, what power the trustee carries, and under what rare circumstances changes are allowed. Make sure everything lines up with state trust codes and statutes.

Funding—Putting Skin in the Game

A trust with nothing in it is just words. You'll need to retitle assets—checking accounts, real estate, stock certificates—so they belong to the trust, not you. Every asset follows its own process under the law. Miss a step and that asset stays exposed.

Running the Trust

Being a trustee means regular duties. Manage investments, file yearly tax returns (Form 1041 for most irrevocable trusts), make timely distributions, and keep the beneficiaries in the loop. The law holds trustees to a high standard. Sloppy records or poor communication rarely end well.

Before You Commit—What You Need to Weigh

Irrevocable means just that. Once you cross this line, you don't get an easy walk back. Think hard before you transfer family land or business interests into one.

Letting Go of the Reins

Assets moved to the trust aren't yours anymore—not for spending, selling, or changing the rules on your own whim. If you have second thoughts after, good luck. Most changes call for unanimous beneficiary consent, or a judge.

Tax Complications

A trust pays its own tax, usually at higher rates and under different rules than individuals. Money the trust earns or sends out can trigger paperwork come April. Attorneys and accountants are worth their fee here, to keep you out of trouble.

Public Benefits and the Five-Year Clock

With Medicaid, what you do today can haunt you five years from now. Transfers to irrevocable trusts count as gifts. If you face the need for care within that window, your eligibility gets delayed. Every trust must be drafted with this federal overlay in mind, especially on the timelines.

The Legal Matrix

The Uniform Trust Code covers most ground, but state statutes and old case law still matter. Laws change. Revisiting your trust with a seasoned attorney keeps it aligned with current rules and your changing needs.

Deciding if the Iron Lock Fits

Irrevocable trusts aren't for the indecisive. You trade flexibility for certainty—fewer surprises, more control after you're gone, but little room to reverse course. If your concerns involve future lawsuits, the rising cost of long-term care, or keeping the family line steady, it can be a solid shield. Weigh your priorities, know the risks. For some, building that wall now is the only sure way to keep the right hands on the legacy later.

Legal counsel helps land the details. State rules rarely forgive the careless or the hasty. If this route fits your goals, set it up with care, and check back as your life or laws change. The trust only works if it matches your intent and the law—no more, no less.

REVOCABLE LIVING TRUSTS: THE PRACTICAL GUIDE

The Nuts and Bolts of a Revocable Living Trust

Paperwork piles up in nearly every home—deeds, account statements, insurance policies. Sooner or later, it raises the same question: who will deal with it all when you're gone, and will those documents end up causing more trouble than good? That's where a revocable living trust comes in. It's not a silver bullet, but it works in ways a will alone can't touch if you value privacy or you've got a complicated setup.

Think of a revocable living trust as a flexible holding cell for your assets—real estate, cash, stocks, you name it. The phrase "living" matters because you set it up while you're alive. "Revocable" means you keep the power. You rewrite, update, or even dismantle it entirely as long as you're of sound mind. This structure has grown on people, especially those wanting to dodge the cost and drag of probate or looking to keep family business out of public files.

The difference between a trust and a will is more than paperwork. Wills wait in limbo until death and must go through the probate court—a process as cumbersome as you'd expect from any government tribunal. Trusts, on the other hand, come alive from the moment you sign and fund them. That control draws people in. You call the shots, you pull the plug, you decide who gets what, and when.

How It Works on the Ground

Setting up a revocable trust is about taking responsibility. The grantor—the person starting the trust—often doubles as the first trustee. It's a way to keep your hands on the steering wheel. Right behind you rides the successor trustee, waiting to take command only if you're incapacitated or dead. The trust spells out what you own, who inherits, and under what terms. Every word in that document carries weight when the time comes.

Getting the Assets Inside—it's Called Funding

Most mistakes happen here. For a trust to do its job, you have to put assets into it. Re-title the house, change the name on your savings, update brokerage records. You'll need to re-record real estate deeds—physical trips to the recorder of deeds office, the notary stamper, the whole bit. Bank accounts mean more forms. The trust only controls what's transferred into it. Leave assets out, and you're right back in probate, despite your best intentions.

Keeping Control as Trustee

You're not boxed in. Amendments are allowed as life shifts. Sell a property, buy another, add a grandchild—you can adjust the trust to fit. None of the ironclad rules of an irrevocable trust; this one bends as you see fit, so long as you have capacity. It's designed for people who expect changes. That's reality for most folks.

When Capacity Fades

Plenty of families avoid difficult conversations, but incapacity happens. In a properly drafted trust, your hand-picked successor trustee can take over without the slow, public spectacle of guardianship court. They pay your bills, handle your property, and follow your instructions—quietly, no judge required.

After Death—What Actually Happens

When you die, your successor trustee pivots from standby to active duty. Their job: round up trust assets, pay off debts and taxes, and distribute what's left according to your written instructions. No court, no probate, no public records office nosing into family matters. Confidentiality is woven into the trust system as an unspoken promise.

Why People Turn to Living Trusts

The stories repeat themselves: A probate case drags on in Jackson County, or an out-of-state property triggers paperwork in two places. Those headaches have pushed people toward revocable living trusts—no smoke, no mirrors, just the promise of less friction for those left behind.

Dodging Probate

Probate isn't just slow; it's a public and expensive process. Lawyers and courts take a cut, newspapers publish your assets. If you move your property into a living trust during your life, probate mostly disappears for those assets. The successor trustee acts with authority. Money and property move quickly, behind closed doors. Heirs benefit in weeks, not months or years.

Keeping Private Matters Private

People value privacy. A will goes through probate, and all the details land in public files—what you owned, what you owed, who fought with whom. In contrast, trusts don't see the inside of a courthouse. Except for the trustee and the named beneficiaries, outsiders see nothing. Privacy is built in, not bolted on.

Planning for the Worst—Not Just Death

Dementia, stroke, a bad accident—sometimes the threat isn't death but incapacity. The trust system lets your chosen backup step in fast. They take over and keep the wheels turning. The courts are circumnavigated. It's a smoother sequence than the fractured realities of state guardianship proceedings.

Owning Property in More Than One State

Maybe you farm in Platte County but own a fishing cabin outside Osage Beach, or a getaway in Arkansas. Property in several states creates a mess at death—"ancillary probate" everywhere you own dirt or timber. Title those out-of-state assets into your trust, and your family won't waste time or cash working multiple court systems. One plan covers it all.

Freedom to Adapt as Life Changes

Life doesn't freeze at the signing table. The law lets you restate, revoke, or refit your
trust as your needs and relationships change. That adaptability stands out. Only assets intentionally added stay controlled—your command, your terms, right to the end.

The Tough Edges and Limits

Revocable living trusts help many, but they have their blind spots. Nothing strips away all risk or responsibility.

Creditors Still Have a Way In

If you're in debt, the trust is not armor. As long as you control the assets, a creditor can still reach them, both while you live and at your death. People looking for tight asset protection need different, tougher strategies—usually irrevocable trusts, which take real control out of your hands but put up a higher wall.

No Tax Magic

Revocable trusts don't shrink your estate for tax purposes. It's all still yours in the eyes of the IRS and your states's taxman. Estate, inheritance, or capital gains taxes stay on the table unless you take special legal steps. The trust is about control and privacy, not savings on taxes by default.

Getting Started Isn't Free or Simple

This isn't fill-in-the-blank law. Setting up a trust requires a good attorney, hours of document review, not a little patience.

Retitling property can mean runs to multiple banks, register of deeds, and the DMV, depending on what you own. If you cut corners or leave assets outside the trust, you may still face probate for missed pieces. People get sloppy; it undercuts everything.

Ongoing Paperwork

If you serve as your own trustee, record-keeping falls on your desk. Every time you buy property or open an account, you'll need to ensure it's correctly titled in the trust's name. Confusion here leads to trouble later. A lawyer with real experience will hand you checklists, but the day-to-day is yours to keep straight.

Who Needs a Revocable Living Trust?

Your reality decides. If you want to hold down costs, shield family business, or own out-of-state real estate, the trust pays for itself. It fits for people with minor children, second marriages, or concerns about incapacity. The world is not simple. The trust gives you tools for complexity, not just size of the estate.

Sometimes, though, simple is enough. A short list of assets, clear heirs, and no privacy concerns—then a will, thoughtful beneficiary designations, and powers of attorney might cover you. But before you draft, ask an estate planning attorney who lives the paperwork each day. It's not worth guessing.

Where You Go from Here

A revocable living trust is practical, private, and powerful when built right. But it's only as good as the care and attention put into its creation and upkeep. Take the time to weigh what matters—to you and your family. Legal work isn't glamorous, but it saves your people headaches and public fights. If you want clarity, start the conversation now. Get a trust drawn up that fits your real life. Do the work up front—so when the time comes, your plan actually delivers.

WILLS: THE REAL RULES FOR MAKING YOURS COUNT

The Nuts and Bolts Behind a Valid Will

You don't get a second shot at a first will. If you die without one, your assets won't go where you thought—they'll follow state-law blueprints, not your own plan. State statutes lay out the rules. Get any piece wrong, expect trouble: arguments, court fights, sometimes the whole document gets thrown out. The only way forward is to know those lines and stick to them. Simple enough, but people trip anyway.

Who the Law Lets Write a Will

If you're 18 or older, or an emancipated minor (not common, but it happens), you can make a will—assuming you're in your right mind when you do. "Sound mind" isn't a phrase lawyers use lightly. You need to know what you own, who your family is, and what leaving a will means. If someone later questions your state of mind, it turns into a battle of facts—doctor's notes, witness stories, all combed over by the court. The law doesn't hand out second chances on competency.

No Telling, No Memory Games—Put It in Writing

Most states doesn't allow you to just tell someone your wishes on your deathbed. *Some do – verify your state law with a licensed attorney* Oral wills, "nuncupative," don't hold water for the general population here. There's the rare exception for active-duty military in very tight circumstances, but the ordinary system is simple: use paper. Scratch out a hand-written will and you're not finished either—not unless you loop in witnesses and do things by statute. Most folks print everything out, but handwritten or typed, the paperwork needs proper eyes on it or it fails.

Tough Stance on Witnesses

For your will to breathe, two adult witnesses must watch you sign your name, or watch you point at your name and admit you signed already. Both need to add their own signatures, standing in that same room, with you alive during the process—that last detail matters more than you'd think.

Those witnesses need to be over 18 and have their wits about them. Best practice: pick witnesses who don't get a dime or any slice of your property under that will. If you let an heir watch and sign, the law punishes that person—they lose the gift. The law lets the will stand if there are two "disinterested" witnesses too, but if you get it wrong, someone's gift may get erased. Ask any probate clerk; this is where people cause delays.

If You Can't Sign, Have a Clear Backup—and a Paper Trail

If your hand shakes or you can't sign for any reason, another person can sign for you, but that move needs to be open—done in your presence, under your direction. It's a red flag moment; judges circle these documents for signs of someone leaning too hard on the testator. If someone else's pen signs your name, make a record of how and why. Stave off the claims of undue influence with details up front.

Turning Your Will Into a Lockbox: Self-Proving in Missouri

Missouri allows you to make a will "self-proving." Here's what that does: if done right, it keeps your witnesses out of court after you're gone, speeds up probate, and makes it much harder for anyone to claim your will is fake or forged. The mechanics are plain: you and your two witnesses sign an affidavit, ideally at that same table, under a notary's watchful eye. The affidavit swears you all followed the law and no one got railroaded. It stays stapled to your will from day one.

Here's what you'll need for the self-proving layer to count:

You, the testator, signing with at least two witnesses present—and the same for the affidavit section. A Missouri notary to stamp every signature. Use language that fits Missouri law—specifically, Section 474.337 of the revised statutes. Get cute with phrasing and it might not count.

The law doesn't force you to self-prove your will, but most lawyers urge it. Makes contests and court headaches less likely. Sometimes, it's the only thing standing between order and chaos.

Landmines in Wills—and How People Still Step on Them

Most folks believe a will is just paperwork and trusted witnesses. That's where mistakes creep in, and those mistakes make probate court busy. A few wrong decisions and your plan unravels fast. State requirements are strict—no room for almosts.

Don't Use an Heir as Witness—It Bites Back

If you let a person named in your will also serve as your witness,
you've built a slow-motion problem. That person risks forfeiting their inheritance if the law isn't strictly followed. Safer bet: use people who don't stand to gain and document presence. Everyone in the room, no shortcuts.

A Will with Missing Signatures Might as Well Be Blank

If any required signature is missing—yours or a witness's—your will's nothing but a story no one can prove. Before that meeting breaks up, every line needs signing, including on the self-proving page if you use one. Otherwise the court tosses it.

Handwritten Is Not Enough—Witnesses Still Matter

Unlike some states, Missouri doesn't recognize holographic wills, no matter how clearly you write your wishes in your own hand. It still needs all legal witnesses, or it's as good as nothing. Hand-written notes found after death spark lawsuits, not certainty.

Wills from Elsewhere—Fine Print Can Save or Doom You

If you wrote your will in another state and move to Missouri, there's a chance the document stands—if it matched the rules where and when you made it. Even so, take it to a Missouri lawyer. Local rules bite. One missed requirement can cost your beneficiaries months in probate, or much worse.

Old Wills Hanging On—A Common, Quiet Error

The law lets you rip up or formally revoke an old will at any time—including by writing a new, complete will. Trying to patch an old one with partial updates or "codicils" isn't usually wise unless you follow every law to the letter—same witnessing, same steps. Play it safe: when in doubt, start fresh and keep the paper trail clean.

Bigger Picture Stuff: Life, Law, and the Will

Life doesn't stay static—neither should your will. The law intersects with life's shocks: marriage, divorce, new children, loss. Each change can turn your clean plan sideways if you don't address it directly.

Marriage and Divorce—Automatic Shifts, Missed Details

If you marry after you write your will, the law still makes room for your new spouse unless you outright say otherwise. Divorce, on the flip side, cuts your former spouse out of your will unless you write it to survive divorce. After big changes, sit down with your document. Letting it ride on old language courts disaster.

Children Arriving Late—Pretermitted Heirs

A child born or adopted after you sign the will is called a "pretermitted heir." The law swings in to protect these kids, giving them a share unless you made it crystal clear you meant to exclude them. If you really mean to disinherit someone, use plain words and document it. The law tries to read between the lines if you don't.

Some Assets Never See Your Will—Plan for That

Certain property slips past your will entirely—property held in joint tenancy, life insurance with named beneficiaries, retirement funds, transfer-on-death and payable-on-death accounts. These move by contract or operation of law. Make sure those designations fit your big plan or they'll rip holes in your intended legacy.

Where to Store It, and Why It Matters

Once your will's signed and stamped, it needs to be where someone you trust can get it.
Courts want the original, not a photocopy. Fireproof safe, bank box, or with your lawyer's files—pick somewhere reliable. Tell your personal representative how to find it, or your best efforts might die in a locked drawer.

Big changes? Change the will. New job, divorce, another child—don't wait. Every update should follow your state's formalities, no shortcuts. Otherwise you leave your heirs with a fight you could have avoided.

Final Word

State will statutes are blunt: do things right, or your last wishes mean nothing. Write it down, sign with witnesses, get your paperwork in order. That's the path to a will that stands up under the hardest scrutiny. The law is there to enforce clarity, not sentiment. Map it out. Leave nothing to luck.

SPECIAL NEEDS TRUSTS: HOW TO PROTECT A LOVED ONE'S FUTURE

The Basics: What a Special Needs Trust Really Does

Picture a parent trying to leave something behind for a child with disabilities. They want to help. The catch: government benefits like Medicaid and SSI have strict rules. Even a small inheritance can push someone over the line, cutting them off from critical support. Those rules do not bend for good intentions.

A Special Needs Trust (SNT) takes a different route. It shields money for someone with a disability without making that person ineligible for public help. The trust holds the assets, not the individual. That legal detail makes all the difference. The trust can then cover expenses Medicaid and SSI won't touch—education, transportation, specialized therapies, a better wheelchair, more control over daily life. The law—federal and state—draws a protective circle around these arrangements, as long as the details are correct. If the trust fits the guidelines, benefits stay intact. The quality of life can improve. That's the principle on paper, but the consequences are real. Without it, inheritances and gifts can cut a loved one off from lifelines they depend on every month.

Trust Types: How the Structure Really Works

It's not one-size-fits-all.
Families have a decision to make up front. The law recognizes three main forms of SNT, each shaped by who owns the assets and how the rules play out over time.

First-Party Trusts: Using the Beneficiary's Own Money

Sometimes a person with disabilities receives a settlement, an inheritance, or has savings in their own name. That's where a First-Party Special Needs Trust comes in. The law says these are only for those under 65 who meet the Social Security Administration's definition of disabled. The price? After the beneficiary dies, any money left pays back the state (whichever state provided Medicaid). Medicaid gets its due. Only then can any remainder go to others in the family.

Third-Party Trusts: Built by Someone Else

Here the money never belonged to the disabled person. A parent, grandparent, or anyone else sets up the trust as part of estate planning. It might be funded by a life insurance policy, a will, or a living trust. There's a key difference: No Medicaid payback required after the beneficiary passes away. Whoever set up the trust decides where any leftovers go. That flexibility matters. The trust can shield and stretch family resources further, without triggering losses in public benefits.

Pooled Trusts: Non-Profit Oversight

Not every family has someone to handle complex fiduciary responsibilities, or the resources for a separate private trust. That's why the law allows pooled trusts, managed by non-profits. Here, individual accounts are pooled for investment but tracked separately. The non-profit runs the fund under tight legal standards. When the beneficiary dies, Medicaid still has a claim, then the non-profit can use any remaining funds to help other beneficiaries, or as directed in the trust agreement. For families with fewer assets, this route often keeps things practical and affordable.

Why Families Choose a Special Needs Trust

SNTs aren't theoretical. The impact lands directly. Trust assets don't count toward the harsh limits that threaten Social Security or Medicaid coverage—so the monthly checks and medical care stay. Beyond that, these trusts deliver what most public programs won't: new dental work, college classes, equipment upgrades, access to summer programs, transportation, a little room to breathe. Trustees, whether a family friend, bank, or non-profit, answer to strict state rules. Their legal duty: act in the beneficiary's best interest, maintain records, and follow detailed reporting requirements. The law commands it, but families feel it most in the small daily improvements to their loved one's life.

For many parents, this brings a steady kind of peace. Even if something happens to them, their child or sibling will not be left exposed or alone. The structure is bendable, too. Optional features—corporate trustee or friendly neighbor, narrow or broad powers, connections to
ABLE accounts—shape the trust for any family's reality.

The Process: Building a Special Needs Trust That Stands Up

Legal Help Isn't Optional

SNT laws can trip up well-meaning families who try to go it alone. Each detail matters: the words of the legal document, the type of trust, who holds the keys as trustee. Getting it wrong—even slightly—could destroy eligibility or open the trust to government clawbacks. An experienced estate-planning attorney knows these hazards. They can match trust structure to the real world, draft the right language, and tie everything to the larger family plan.

DIY kits and web templates promise savings but often create messes. Missing Medicaid clauses, flawed payout instructions, or confused funding can cost much more than a legal bill. Correcting a bad trust usually means probate court, lost benefits, or both.

Who Can Be Trustee?

The work isn't just legal—someone has to run the trust. This trustee might be a family member, friend, bank, or non-profit board. The law expects them to be organized, unbiased, and diligent. Every year, the trustee must account for each payment and investment. Sloppy records or friendly shortcuts can trigger state audits and risk benefits for the disabled person. The best trustees have a head for details and a clear sense of duty, not just affection or good intentions.

Funding and Running the Trust: Daily Details Matter

The trust can be funded at any time—immediately, or through a will or insurance policy after the parents die. This shields the disabled person from a direct inheritance, which could upend government support. After funding, the trustee must direct payments not to the beneficiary
but to service providers or for approved expenses: rent, medical gear, tuition, therapies. Cash handed straight to the beneficiary counts as income and can wreck SSI. Every transaction must be documented, with Medicaid and SSI rules in mind. Trustees that get lazy or try to take shortcuts face stiff government scrutiny.

State Particular Rules: No Room for Error

Agencies treat these trusts as exempt from asset limits only if the details line up. Improper payments or loose reporting can flip the trust from asset to liability—disqualifying the beneficiary from needed programs almost overnight. The Department of Social Services audits SNTs and demands detailed accountings that hold up under questioning. First-party and pooled trusts require exact Medicaid payback language or the trust simply does not work. Even the timing of deposits or certain gifts has to be handled exactly, or else penalties kick in. In some cases, a local probate court intervenes—especially for minors or adults under guardianship. Oversight is real, and families need to plan for it.

When to Set Up a SNT: Signs and Signals

Families act before there's a problem. If a loved one with disabilities may inherit money, win a legal settlement, or receive gifts beyond the government asset cap, a Special Needs Trust buys breathing room. This also matters when parents want peace about long-term care or siblings plan to contribute later—any situation where private funds touch public benefits triggers the same risk. Early planning is the best chance for stability.

But the job's not finished once the trust is built. Periodic reviews, with updates for new
laws or family realities, close loopholes and keep government programs secure.

Getting Started: The Moves That Matter

The process is stepwise and practical. First, assess your family's reality—medical, financial, and social gaps included. Then choose the trust type: first-party if the disabled person owns the assets, third-party for family contributions, or pooled for lower balances and specialized management. Pay an attorney to draft a trust that fits your state's's precise legal language. Nominate a trustee who can do the record-keeping and decision-making. Set up the funding, then coordinate with other estate plans and insurance policies. Finally, teach everyone involved about the rules —one slip can bring consequences that last years.

For families with a vulnerable member, the SNT is more than paperwork. It's a shield. Set up correctly, it lets a loved one keep their benefits, stretch their support, and hold on to some independence—no matter what changes tomorrow may bring.

IF YOU LEAVE A CHILD'S INHERITANCE WITHOUT A TRUST

What Really Happens When a Minor Inherits

A parent dies. The paperwork points to the kids. Family expects things to fall into place, assets passing smoothly through a will. But the law steps in with its own set of rules—especially when those heirs are under 18. Most families don't see the tripwire until it snaps shut. If there's no trust, the law doesn't let a minor take the wheel, no matter what the will says. The state has built a fence around minor's inheritances—part shelter, part bureaucratic barrier—and it's easy to miss until you hit it.

Most state call anyone under 18 a minor. If a parent leaves money or property directly to a child—through a will, a retirement account's beneficiary line, or just by dying without a plan—the system reroutes everything. Courts and banks won't hand the keys to a kid. The entire asset pool goes under court supervision. This isn't just a formality. It's a process: guardianship papers, conservatorship filings, and a judge's ongoing thumbprint on a family's financial life until the child turns legal age. It's supposed to protect, but it's far from simple or quick.

Guardians, Conservators, and the Machinery of Probate Court

The law doesn't trust a child with money or property.

Someone else has to step in. Two specific jobs get appointed: the guardian (taking care of the person—where they live, their health, school, and well-being) and the conservator (handling every dollar and deed of the inheritance). Sometimes it's one person wearing both hats. Sometimes not. Each has a legal job to do.

If there's no clear direction in your will, the probate court makes the call. Relatives usually get first shot, but even then, it's the judge's decision. The conservator has to file a petition, attend a hearing, and usually promise—often with a bond—to play it straight. After that, the clock starts. Every year, the conservator sends an accounting to the court: what's spent, what's invested, what's left. Can't sell property, tap big accounts, or take big risks without showing it to a judge first. The conservator gets paid (a little), but it all comes from the child's share. So do the court costs. So do the lawyer's bills.

If you're picturing a smooth track, erase it. Families get mired in paperwork, waiting rooms, and slow court calendars. Buying new school clothes or covering a medical bill could mean filing for permission. If the family moves out of state, things can get even more tangled, with court still clinging to authority like a stubborn thornbush.

The Toll of Court Control

This structure looks protective on paper. In real life, it can grind families down. Every decision with real money behind it hits a wall of court approval. Hearings can stretch weeks into months. Even urgent needs—medical care, therapy, sports fees—can hang in limbo. Relatives, sometimes at odds, may fight over who gets control. Their battle unfolds in public. The courthouse file shows every detail of the inheritance, where it goes, how fast it burns. Anyone willing can read it, making the family's money matters a matter of public record.

Disputes over conservatorship are settled out in the open. Arguing relatives, expensive lawyers, all of them answering to the system. The child's future gets wrapped up in legal tape and court schedules. And the assets—meant to buy opportunity and security—slowly shrink from all the fees and waiting.

The Clock Strikes 18: A Hard Transition

There's a deadline built into this machine. When the minor turns 18, the door swings open. The conservatorship ends. Whatever's left passes, in one shot, to the now-legal adult. No training required. No guardrails. Every dollar and asset lands on the desk of someone whose main experience with the system has been telling people their age.

Most 18-year-olds stand at the threshold of adulthood with little real sense for money. $10,000 or $1,000,000—it all lands in the same checking account, ready to use. No law stops them from burning through it. Nobody has to coach, pause, or even ask questions. The state considers its duty finished. That's how windfalls blow away, or worse, get tangled by fast-talkers and distant "friends." Houses, farms, businesses—if those are part of the inheritance—they go too. There's no slow handover, no mentoring, no official pause for second thoughts.

And since the conservatorship records are public, word spreads quickly about any young person who's just come into money. That, too, brings its own risks.

Smarter Approaches: Planning That Fits The Law

The default system—court, conservator, public record—rarely matches a family's hopes or the realities of raising a child through loss. There are better ways, if you use them on purpose. Each comes with its own requirements and trade-offs.

Trusts: The Private, Controlled Option

The cleanest solution is a revocable living trust. The parent creates it while alive, choosing a trusted adult (or even a pro) to manage everything after death. They spell out the plan: wait until twenty-five for access, pay college expenses from the trust, release funds in steps, cover health needs, maybe buy a used car for work. The rules fit the family, not just the court's template. The trustee follows the playbook written by the parent, not by a judge. Learn more about why a trust for your child should mature with your child and understanding the basics of trusts in estate planning.

There's no court poking into the family's business unless trouble brews. The details stay private. A trustee still answers to basic legal duties but isn't burdened by annual court reporting unless someone demands it. The expense, the delays, and the public record disappear. Most families never look back after putting this in place.

UTMA Accounts: Simple, with a Catch

State Uniform Transfers to Minors Act lets parents or others move money or property for a child outside the court system. They pick a custodian ("John Doe, as custodian for Jane Doe under the UTMA"), and that adult handles everything, without court oversight. It works well for smaller inheritances or where the situation doesn't call for long-term guardrails. It's quick. It's cheap. No annual filings.

But when the child turns 21—or sooner, if the original paperwork says so—they get it all, free and clear. No strings, no delay. You can't extend oversight past that point or customize the payout. Some families can live with that limit. Others can't risk it, not with bigger sums or complicated needs.

Watch the Beneficiary Lines

Bank accounts, life insurance, retirement plans—these often let you name a direct beneficiary. Some parents just write in a minor's name, thinking the payout will be fast. But banks and insurance companies refuse to cut a check to anyone under 18. They demand proof of a conservatorship or a UTMA arrangement before releasing funds. This surprises families every year, especially after a loss.

If you want to avoid probate drags and conservatorship headaches, look at every beneficiary designation. Make sure it matches your wider plan. Let the trust or UTMA handle the payout. Miss one of these, and the system steps right back onto the field.

The Straight Path: Protect What You Build

Each state's default system—wills, intestate rules, and court-supervised processes—puts families at the mercy of red tape and public oversight. It drains time and money and offers little guidance once the child is legally grown. Most parents want more: control, privacy, someone they trust overseeing the money, and a plan that holds together when stress hits.

The law offers the tools, but you have to pick them up. A living trust centers the plan around family, not bureaucracy. A UTMA account works for simpler, smaller legacies. Either way, don't leave the machinery on autopilot. Consult an actual estate attorney. Make a plan that fits your child, avoids needless court control, and keeps the family's future within the family's hands.

SECTION 3: LIFE STAGES

ESTATE PLANNING: HOW IT WORKS FOR NEW PARENTS WITHOUT A WILL

When new parents die without a will, the state's intestacy laws dictate who inherits their assets and, critically, who will raise their minor children. This means a probate court makes decisions that could have been made by the parents, often leading to unintended outcomes and significant stress for surviving family members.

You just had a baby. Congratulations. Now, think about the unthinkable. If something happens to both you and your partner, who raises your child? What happens to your house, your savings, your life insurance? If you haven't put a will or other estate plan in place, the law decides. Not you. This isn't fearmongering; it's the reality new parents face without proper estate planning.

The Hard Truth: Intestacy

Dying "intestate" simply means you died without a valid will. Most people think this means the state takes everything. Not exactly. What it means is the law has a default plan for your property. It's a one-size-fits-all approach, and it almost never fits your family's specific needs.

For new parents, this gets complicated fast. Your assets, your bank accounts, your investments – they don't automatically go to your minor child. Instead, intestacy laws dictate a specific order of inheritance. If you have a spouse and children, your spouse typically inherits the first $20,000 of your estate, plus half of the remaining balance. Your children inherit the other half. If you have no spouse, your children inherit everything. Sounds simple, right? It's not. These assets don't go directly to your child. They can't. A minor child cannot legally own property outright. A court must step in.

This entire process happens through probate court. It's public. It's often slow. And it can be expensive. A judge, a stranger, will oversee the distribution of your life's work. This is the first major roadblock for new parents who haven't planned.

Who Raises Your Kids? Guardianship without a Will

This is the most critical issue for new parents. Your biggest worry, and rightly so, is who will care for your child if you're gone. Without a will, you don't get to choose. The court does. This is a guardianship proceeding, separate from asset distribution.

When there's no will naming a guardian, any interested party can petition the probate court to be appointed. This could be a grandparent, an aunt, an uncle, or even a close family friend. The judge, again, a stranger, makes the final decision based on what they believe is in "the best interest of the child."

This "best interest" standard is broad. It can lead to family disputes, arguments over who is most suitable, and ultimately, a drawn-out legal battle. Imagine your grieving family fighting in court over who gets to raise your child. It's a painful scenario. This is not the legacy you want to leave. A simple will allows you to name the person or people you trust most to raise your children, avoiding this potential conflict entirely. It's the most important reason to act.

Your Assets: Where Do They Go?

As mentioned, if you die intestate, your minor children will inherit a portion of your estate. But they won't get direct access to it. The law requires that a conservator be appointed by the probate court to manage these funds until your child turns 18. This conservator is typically the same person appointed as guardian, but not always.

The conservator has a legal duty to manage the money for the child's benefit. This means paying for their education, health, maintenance, and support. However, every expenditure must be approved by the court. It's a bureaucratic hurdle. It also means your child will receive all remaining assets in a lump sum the day they turn 18. Many 18-year-olds are not equipped to handle a significant inheritance responsibly. There's no ongoing guidance, no staggered distribution, no control over how the money is spent.

You worked hard for that money. You likely envision it being used for college, starting a business, or a down payment on a home. Without a plan, you lose all control over that vision. A trust, for example, allows you to set specific conditions for how and when your child receives their inheritance, ensuring it's used wisely and protected for their future.

The Probate Process: An Unwanted Burden

If you die without a will, your estate will almost certainly go through probate. Probate is the legal process of proving a will is valid (if one exists) and then administering the estate – identifying assets, paying debts, and distributing what's left to heirs.

When there's no will, the court appoints a "personal representative" (sometimes called an administrator) to manage your estate. This person is often a family member, but they may have no experience with legal or financial matters. They'll have to navigate court filings, communicate with creditors, and distribute assets according to intestacy statutes. It's a significant responsibility, especially for someone who is already grieving your loss.

Probate can tie up assets for months, sometimes even years. It incurs legal fees, court costs, and administrative expenses. These costs reduce the inheritance your family ultimately receives. More importantly, it adds immense stress and a bureaucratic nightmare for your loved ones during an already difficult time. Proper estate planning, even a basic will, can significantly streamline this process or even help your family avoid probate entirely.

Why a Will Isn't Enough (But It's a Start)

A will is essential. It lets you name guardians for your minor children. It designates a personal representative to handle your estate. It dictates how your assets are distributed. For new parents, it's the bare minimum. But it's not the complete picture.

Even with a will, many assets may still go through probate. Property held solely in your name, without a beneficiary designation, will likely be subject to the probate process. This is where other estate planning tools come into play. A revocable living trust, for instance, allows you to transfer ownership of your assets into the trust during your lifetime. When you pass away, the assets in the trust can be distributed to your beneficiaries without going through probate court. This saves time, money, and maintains privacy.

Beyond wills and trusts, durable powers of attorney are critical. These documents allow you to designate someone to make financial and healthcare decisions for you if you become incapacitated. Without them, your family might have to go to court to get a guardianship or conservatorship over you, which is another costly and time-consuming process. Estate planning isn't just about what happens after you're gone; it's also about protecting you and your family if you can't make decisions yourself.

Taking Control: Essential Steps for New Parents

It's clear that doing nothing leaves your family vulnerable. Taking control is straightforward. Here are the fundamental steps new parents should consider:

Draft a Will:
This is the starting point. Name guardians for your minor children. Designate a personal representative. Specify how your tangible personal property should be distributed. This single document prevents the state from making your most personal decisions.

Consider a Revocable Living Trust:
For many families, a trust offers superior control and privacy. It avoids probate for assets held within the trust, provides for ongoing management of assets for your children, and allows for staggered distributions, preventing an 18-year-old from inheriting a fortune all at once.

Review Beneficiary Designations:
Life insurance policies, retirement accounts (401ks, IRAs), and transfer-on-death (TOD) or payable-on-death (POD) accounts pass directly to your named beneficiaries, outside of probate. Ensure these are up-to-date and name contingent beneficiaries.

Execute Durable Powers of Attorney:
These documents are for your incapacity. A Durable Power of Attorney for Healthcare names someone to make medical decisions. A Durable Power of Attorney for Finances names someone to manage your money. Both are crucial for protecting you and your family while you're still living.

Talk to Your Family:
Discuss your choices for guardians and personal representatives with the people you've named. Ensure they understand and are willing to serve. Transparency prevents surprises later.

Don't Wait: Protect Your Family's Future

Having a new baby changes everything. Your priorities shift. Protecting that child becomes paramount. Estate planning is a crucial part of that protection. It provides peace of mind, knowing that if the unthinkable happens, your family will be cared for according to your wishes, not a default state statute.

Don't let the complexity stop you. Your family deserves that protection. It's an investment in their future, and your legacy.

For new parents, understanding Estate Planning: How It Works for New Parents Without a Will is not just legal advice; it's a critical act of love and responsibility. Without a plan, the law dictates who raises your children, how your assets are managed, and how your estate is probated. This often leads to unnecessary stress, expense, and potential family conflict. Take control. Protect your family's future by establishing a comprehensive estate plan.

TURNING 18: THE REAL CONSEQUENCES —AND THE LEGAL PAPERS YOU NEED

Eighteen arrives without much fanfare. A driver's license, maybe cake, a few off-handed remarks about "adulthood." But, the ground shifts that day. You step over a line—by law, you're fully separated from your parents. You can rent your own place, see the doctor alone, sign a lease, borrow money, or choose your treatments. The flip side: your parents don't get to know your grades, check your accounts, or speak for you in the emergency room without your say-so. It's liberating, and risky, all at once. The only way to handle that new exposure: put the right legal tools in your pocket before real life backs you into a corner.

What Happens When You Turn 18?

One minute, mom or dad can call the school to ask about your attendance. Next day, no dice. The "age of majority" law draws a hard boundary at 18. After this birthday, nobody—even family—has legal permission to get your records, make health choices, or handle your money unless you put it in writing. It's a clean break, whether you still sleep under their roof or have already shipped out for boot camp. Phone calls won't fix it. Front desk workers, school registrars, and bank tellers can't legally budge without your signed consent.

This change is sharp. A hospital can't talk to your parents if you're unconscious. The college won't hand out your grades when finals tank, even if mom is footing the bill. Move-out day, or enlistment, or returning home from a dorm, doesn't matter—the rules trail you. State law is particular and strict, so if you plan to let anyone in on your personal business, you have to give them a legal seat at the table.

The Documents That Matter Right Now

No one likes paperwork, but, a grown child without the right documents is standing in the rain without a coat. Here's what actually counts when you turn 18:

Durable Power of Attorney for Healthcare

Accidents happen, sometimes fast. With a Durable Power of Attorney for Healthcare, you pick someone—usually a parent—to talk to doctors and make choices if you're knocked out, in surgery, or otherwise unable to say what you want. No one steps in by default. If you don't have this, decisions get stalled, and the hospital locks everyone out. This form clears barriers, lets your chosen person react while everyone else waits in the lobby.

No hospital will risk breaking HIPAA or state privacy law. A signed healthcare power of attorney is a key. Without it, your voice is gone when you need it most.

HIPAA Authorization

Doctors can't spill a word about your injuries, diagnosis, or prescriptions unless you've spelled out who can know. HIPAA is absolute here. A young adult in a car wreck, or fighting an infection at the hospital, may have no family updates unless they've pre-approved someone with a proper HIPAA release on file. Without this slip of paper, your closest people are left guessing at the door, or piecing together rumors. Clinics and ERs all demand the signed form before they pick up the phone.

Durable Power of Attorney for Finances

Banker won't even look at your parent if your name's on the account, not theirs. That can get ugly fast if you're in another country, hospitalized, or just offline. A Durable Financial Power of Attorney lets someone you trust pay your tuition, renew your lease, pull together loan info, or move money when you can't. Without it, everyone's hands are tied. State law requires careful language—don't guess at this one. If there's a screw-up, it's you who pays the price down the road.

Advance Directive (Living Will)

No one wants to picture a ventilator, but life turns without warning. An advance directive—call it a living will if you like—tells doctors what measures you want if things get dire: feeding tubes, resuscitation, all-in or none. These decisions are yours only if you put them in black and white, early. Hospitals here will follow it. Families, too, are spared midnight arguments and second-guessing if your choices are written down and clear.

FERPA Release

At any college, privacy rules are ironclad. Turn 18 or enroll, and your education records slam shut—no more parent access by default, not for grades, schedules, or tuition. A FERPA Release is the way of letting you pick who can see your transcripts and payments. This form usually sits with the registrar. Handy if you want your parents to keep an eye on scholarships, or to settle a bill when you're out of range. Otherwise, they're out of the loop, frustrated, and sometimes facing real trouble getting you the help you need.

Last Will and Testament

You might think you don't own enough to bother, but the state doesn't care if your estate is just a half-full savings account or a hand-me-down car. With no will, the state carves up your property while loved ones guess what you'd have chosen. If you have a child, the stakes double—you name a guardian, or a judge does. Digital accounts and keepsakes matter, too. A clear will, kept simple or detailed, prevents most of the ugly fights nobody wants to see after you're gone.

Getting It Done—And Keeping It Fresh

This isn't complicated if you go about it the right way, but mistakes cost time and cash later. Get everyone together around a table. Have the tough conversations—who gets what responsibility, who you trust to handle money or health decisions, and what you want left private. Don't wing it. Lawyers who know estate and adulthood law can steer you clear of red tape, make sure each document lines up with state rules, and that every signature and notarization counts.

- Talk it out—
  Don't leave anyone guessing who should act as your "agent" and when. Spell it out from the start.
- Use a lawyer—
  The laws get granular. Details about notarizing or witnessing a will or power of attorney matter. One error, and your wishes get tossed in court.
- Control your copies—
  The originals need to be safe. Agents and institutions should have easy access to official versions, not just photographs or memory.
- Check and update—
  People move, change schools, split from families, or switch relationships. If your circle changes, your documents need to keep up.

This is the handoff between childhood and real independence. Laying out these papers forces hard thinking and clear communication. The law makes no exceptions. Getting these documents in place is a last act of protection—sometimes for your sake, sometimes for the ones you're leaving behind.

Adulthood: Common Questions, Simple Answers

Do parents lose all rights when their child turns 18?

Yes. Most states recognize 18 as the cutoff. Healthcare, academics, and money—every category needs written approval for ongoing access. No wiggle room, unless the adult child signs the right release or power of attorney.

Does every young adult really need all these papers?

Maybe not every single one. But the basics—healthcare power of attorney, HIPAA release, and a way to manage finances—form a safety net. College-bound kids almost always need a FERPA form. Even if you own little, a will keeps control simple and confusion low.

Can you prep these documents before turning 18?

No. The law won't honor adult documents before age 18, but you can meet with a lawyer and have everything ready to sign the day the birthday arrives. No gap, no scramble.

What if you never get around to these documents?

If nothing's in place when a crisis hits, families get locked out—hospitals stay silent, finances freeze, grades go undisclosed. Sometimes the only option left is going to court, chasing guardianship, and losing precious time.

Turning 18 isn't just another number. With these documents lined up, families won't be left scrambling if disaster knocks. No one plans for the worst. The ones who've seen it know better than to wait.

ESTATE PLANNING FOR ENTREPRENEURS: KEEPING YOUR COMPANY, AND YOUR FAMILY, ON SOLID GROUND

You start a business. It takes years—maybe decades—of early mornings, tight cash, long meetings that spill into dinner. Bit by bit, what you build takes on its own shape and weight. Then success arrives, but it never travels alone. Every step forward adds new questions. What happens to all this if you get sick, leave, or die? Who's ready to lead, and who gets left out in the cold? If your name's on the sign, you'll need to answer these questions for yourself, not just for now but for everyone counting on you. Estate planning is the tool for owners who mean to stay in control—before someone else makes the call.

Walking Both Sides: Family and Company Bound Up Together

An entrepreneur wears too many hats to count. You might be paying your staff, coaching Little League, and handling customers before breakfast. The company's future does not separate from your own. As you grow, your personal nest egg weaves itself through the same bank accounts and legal papers as the shop or firm or factory you run. This tangle is why business owners can't use off-the-shelf estate plans. Your plan has to tie your legacy to the business you've built and protect both angles at once.

- The basics aren't complicated, but what you put off can blindside your family and partners:
- A will and trust drafted for both your business and your household.
- Business succession terms in plain English—not just for death, but if you're laid up or leave suddenly Financial tools to trim taxes and make sure cash is available when it's needed most
- Incapacity documents: someone able—and named —to carry the load if you can't
- Risk shields to keep lawsuits, divorces, or creditors from turning your assets into a scrap pile

Nothing good comes from ignoring these talks. The law will step in by default. The court, not you, will decide who manages the company, who gets what, and when. You might care about protecting the business, but the law cares about following the code.

Keeping the Lights On: Succession and Continuity

In every family business or partnership, continuity matters. If nobody's ready when an owner falls out, the whole structure sags. Sometimes companies land in chaos when a founder dies; other times, they're quietly sold off for less than their worth. The only way to avoid this is to spell out what happens next, in writing, before it's too late.

Passing the Torch

Most owners hope the business stays in the family or lands in known hands. Picking a successor—and preparing them to lead—deserves more than a formality. If your kids won't take over, or your spouse never wanted the job, look to a co-owner, trusted manager, or even a third party. Each path brings different paperwork and tax results. Guesswork isn't a plan.

The Gears That Turn It

Business attorneys use a toolbox for these transitions:

- Buy-sell agreements:
  Set fair terms for selling an ownership stake after death, disability, or pulling up stakes. Life insurance can cover the cash so nobody's forced to sell at a discount.
- Living trusts:
  Shift business interests outside of probate—less fighting, more privacy, less delay.
- Operating or shareholder agreements:
  Spell out what happens with votes, shares, and control if an owner disappears.
- Gifting:
  Edge out tax burdens by giving away pieces little by little, while shaping who's truly in charge.

None of these mean a thing if kept in a desk drawer. Partnerships, especially, need annual check-ins. Life changes, and the paperwork has to keep up.

The Right Documents: Laying Down the Roadmap

No owner should rely on a single sheet or handshake. These are the anchors:

- **Last Will and Testament:**
  Breaks down who gets what. Skip this, and state law carves up your work according to its script, not yours.
- **Revocable Living Trust:**
  Bypasses public probate, keeps business details quiet,

and can keep things moving if you're gone or incapacitated.

- **Durable Power of Attorney:**
Names someone who can pay bills, sign documents, and keep the engines running if you can't.
- **Health Care Directive:**
Decides who speaks for you with doctors and hospitals when you can't speak up yourself.
- **Business succession papers:**
All the agreements drafted for your company—from buy-sell to job duties in a pinch.

Every document should fit both your personal needs and the beating heart of your company. Mishmash drafting creates gaps —gaps create fights. Clean coordination is key.

Tax Pressure and Keeping Cash in Reach

Most entrepreneurs' wealth isn't in their bank account; it's in the business—equipment, contracts, goodwill, receivables. When federal estate taxes come calling, they don't take "It's tied up in assets" as an answer. Current federal exemptions might seem generous, but Congress writes new laws when the wind shifts. Don't count on things staying the same.

Valuation and Getting to Dollars

If you don't know what your business is worth, you can't plan for taxes or sales. Get an outside appraisal, not an industry guess. If the tax bill comes due and all the cash is stuck in inventory or accounts receivable, survivors could be forced to sell fast and cheap. Life insurance, owned by a trust, can supply liquidity fast—no fire sale required.

Cutting Back the Tax Bite

Owners use a few common tools:

- Gradually transfer ownership through gifts, using IRS exemptions year by year

- Move shares into irrevocable trusts, keeping future growth outside your taxable estate
- Use a family limited partnership or LLC to centralize control and qualify for valuation discounts as you pass shares along

A lawyer, accountant, and financial planner working together makes this much less painful. Go it alone and you risk a costly mistake—sometimes at the worst moment.

The Safety Net: Protecting Your Family, Defending the Business

Some risks you see coming—a diagnosis, a slow decline, a family feud. Others hit out of nowhere. Illness, sudden loss, or disputes can put both family and business in a tailspin. Estate planning steps in as a defensive wall. It doesn't just split your property; it empowers someone who can act, sign, and steer when you're not able.

Details You Can't Ignore

Every business entity comes with its own transfer process at death or incapacity. Corporate stock, LLC units, partnership rights—each have separate statutes, procedures, and risks. The state may not tax your estate directly, but the IRS still may (this changes with politics far too often). Keep an eye on changes. If your company leases space, holds permits, or signs contracts in your name, those too need careful review. Don't give a judge a reason to shut down daily operations while your heirs argue.

Powers of attorney and advance directives are the levers that can keep a business moving. Ignore these, and one hospitalization or car wreck can freeze payroll and trigger a dozen headaches. The law only protects those who bother to update and sign the right papers.

Estate Plans Don't Stand Still—Neither Should You

Your first estate plan won't be your last. Growth, personnel changes, marriage, divorce, or branching into new territories can all shift the ground beneath you. Every major change means it's time to sit down and review your plan. Miss an update, and the documents on file might say something you'd never agree to now.

- Bringing in or buying out an owner
- Making a big acquisition or selling a division
- Shifting the balance sheet value significantly
- A birth, death, marriage, or divorce in the family tree
- Moving your residence across state lines
- Mark your calendar for an annual review. Even one outmoded clause or missing name can muddy the waters for your family—and risk the business itself.

The Right Advisors for the Job

Running a company comes with enough headaches without legal paperwork catching you off guard. Link up with a local attorney who knows the statutes and the realities of running a private business in this state. Bring in a CPA and financial advisor who can talk straight to the numbers. Together, they help pin down a plan that locks in your choices and locks out needless trouble.

Every owner builds a legacy, but only a handful keep a grip on it past their lifetime. Good planning isn't glamorous, but the alternative—watching your work drift away in court—never is. Let your plan grow as the company grows. That's how you make sure your name means something, long after you're gone.

WHY BUSINESS OWNERS CAN'T RELY ON A WILL ALONE

Why a Business Changes the Estate Planning Game

Owning a business means you have more to worry about than just what happens to your house or checking account after you're gone. A will might tell the court who gets your personal belongings, but it shrinks quickly when it comes to real business questions—who keeps the lights on, who takes over the payroll, who actually runs the shop the day after you aren't able. These problems lie beneath the surface. If a business owner dies or becomes incapacitated and hasn't mapped out a real estate plan, what was a steady operation can stall out fast. Employees look for leadership that isn't there. Families face uncertainty about money and control. Nobody's job is safe.

Business interests don't behave like basic property. No one sells a slice of their company as easily as cashing out a savings bond. Business holdings often come with partners, silent investors, and managers—all with stakes. Drop a simple will into that mix, and you've only answered where "ownership" winds up, not who keeps the gears turning. The law has plenty to say about business succession, taxes, and probate. None of it is simple, and most of it can't be solved by a single document.

What a Will Doesn't Cover in Business

Plenty of folks think a will fixes everything—passes down the house, the truck, the business. That view misses the cracks. A will lets you name inheritors, appoint an executor, maybe even point out who should watch the kids. But when your "asset" is a living business, with employees, accounts payable, vendor contracts, and partners with skin in the game, a will is a leaky bucket.

First, wills wind up in probate here—sometimes public, sometimes months long, always slow. Your business could grind to a halt. Checks don't get signed, decisions don't get made, authority is blurry. The executor you pick in your will might be a good person, but that doesn't mean they know how to handle client disputes or bank loans. Meanwhile, any friction between heirs or co-owners threatens to pull the operation apart. Even a small dispute can snowball, and every day that ticks by means lost momentum or revenue.

To make it worse, most companies have bylaws or operating agreements with strict rules. Think buy-sell clauses or transfer limits built right into the original paperwork. These rules often override what's said in your will. Fail to sync your estate plan with the business's own set of laws, and your family could end up boxed out by partners—or forced to sell at a bad price just to clear probate.

Real Planning: Succession, Not Just Names on a Paper

If you want the business to survive—not just your name on a deed but actual continuity—you need more. Succession planning deals with real issues: passing authority, stopping infighting, and mapping out how the pieces shift when you're no longer around. Tools like buy-sell agreements, living trusts, and powers of attorney don't just fill out a lawyer's checklist; they fill in the gaps a basic will can't touch.

The Buy-Sell Agreement's Muscle

Every serious business has some form of buy-sell agreement. This is the contract that says what happens to your share of the business if you die, retire, or get sick. It spells out who has the right to buy, what price they pay, and how it all goes down. It acts like insurance against chaos. With a buy-sell in place—and with proper funding like life insurance to pay for it—your partners aren't left scrambling for money, and your family doesn't wind up holding a piece of paper they can't cash or manage.

Skip this step and you're leaving your loved ones with ownership in name, but no path to use it. The company may stall or split. Sometimes, a forced sale follows with no real preparation.

Trusts for Privacy and Control

Many owners turn to a revocable living trust to skip probate and keep business dealings private. By shifting your business interest into a trust now, you set up a system so a successor trustee can step in the moment something happens to you—no courts, no waiting. Control passes smoothly.

Owners with tangled organizational charts or plans to wind down the business get extra mileage out of a business trust. Set the terms for who manages, who gets paid, even how and when to sell off business assets. It's all right there, in writing, managed by the trustee you pick.

Powers of Attorney Keep the Wheels Turning

Plenty of businesses rest on one set of shoulders. If that person is gone, even for a few days, everything halts. A durable power of attorney for finance gives someone you trust permission to keep the place running—pay bills, sign contracts, handle the books. The law lets you make this as narrow or broad as you want. Miss this and, if you're suddenly incapacitated, your people could face legal red tape for weeks, with contracts unsigned and vendors unpaid. Sometimes it takes months for the court to sort it out. That's enough time for a competitor to move in or for key employees to walk.

Review and update these powers regularly, especially alongside business documents. Every gap is an open door for confusion.

Tax Landmines and Protecting What You've Built

Business owners shouldn't just plan for control—they need to plan for tax and creditor risks too. Some states skip state inheritance taxes, but big enough business interests can bring in federal estate or gift tax headaches. When a plan isn't nailed down, your heirs might be forced to dump business assets just to pay Uncle Sam—often at a loss.

Smart owners build in protection. Family limited partnerships, LLCs, irrevocable trusts—all methods for shielding your hard-earned equity from creditors and minimizing tax burn. Each tool, when set up right, locks away value for the people you actually choose.

Aligning Your Estate Plan with the Business Rulebook

Overlooking the gap between your will and your company's own agreements is a classic error.
Courts don't guess—they follow the company documents first. A partnership contract or LLC agreement with a buyout clause trumps your trust or your will every time.

Make sure your estate plan references those same agreements. Spot new risks after major business changes—a merger, a divorce, a new child—and tighten up both sets of papers. The less left unclear, the fewer headaches for your family or remaining partners.

Handling Family, and Avoiding Messy War Stories

Families don't always get along, and business rarely makes them friendlier. Sometimes multiple relatives work inside the business, sometimes none of them care or know how to lead. Call out these realities up front, while you still can.

Lay out who manages, who inherits, and who interacts with outside partners. Some problems can't be settled with words, so use mediation or arbitration clauses right in the core documents. These are faster and keep disputes out of court, where everyone loses.

When Selling or Closing Up Shop Makes Sense

Some owners know the business should end with them. Sometimes continuing is a mistake. If you want the business sold or wound down, state it clear—who sells, how, and who handles the money. Trusts or powers of attorney can carry out your orders, protect value, and head off fire sales or arguments between unprepared heirs.

For closely held companies or licensed professions extra compliance steps apply.
Build those requirements into your instructions.

Planning Done Right Means Survival—Not Just for the Business

Relying on a will alone is a risk nobody should take. A complete plan means laying tracks with buy-sell agreements, trusts, and real powers of attorney. Keeping those documents in lockstep with your business's bylaws and partnership agreements keeps headaches to a minimum, not just for you but for everyone tied to the company's future.

Act today, not tomorrow. The cost of waiting is usually highest when nobody expects the bill.

ESTATE PLANNING WHEN YOU HAVE YOUNG KIDS: GETTING AHEAD OF PROBATE

Every parent with young kids runs into the same crossroads: how do we build something steady for them if something happens to us? Paperwork is only part of it. You're not just splitting up property or listing names. You're choosing who'll stand in your shoes and make sure your kids have both care and cash if you're not around. Most parents don't realize how hard the court process, called probate, can hit families with young children. The clock ticks slower after a loss. Money can get stuck in limbo. Kids' school fees, groceries, rent—nothing waits for paperwork. Knowing your state rules and the workarounds means you get to call the shots, not a courthouse. Plan early, and you save your family months of red tape right when they need answers, not obstacles.

Understanding Probate—and Why Parents Should Avoid It

Probate sounds clinical, but it's a grind. The state checks your will, sorts your assets, settles debts, and finally divvies up what's left. The court appoints someone to run the show, tracks every penny, collects court fees and attorney payments, and makes sure things go by the book—even if the book takes a year to read. Even for a small estate , expect months. Costs climb fast. Paper cuts add up.

If you've got kids under 18, probate creates special headaches. The law doesn't let children inherit assets straight-up. A court-ordered conservator or guardian steps in—and almost everything needs court sign-off. Emergency dental visit? The court decides if you get the money. Want to use your inheritance for summer camp? You wait for a judge. If there's no will or trust, someone else picks who raises your kids and manages their money. The system means well, but it doesn't know your kids or your story.

The fix starts before the crisis. Plan ahead, name your people, lay out your wishes. Skipping probate doesn't mean cutting corners. The law offers tools to do this clean, legal, and fast for the people you care about most.

Tools to Spare Your Kids the Wait

Every state gives families several ways to keep assets out of probate. Each tool fits some properties better than others. You decide who's in charge and how your kids' future is shaped, not a stranger at a hearing.

Revocable Living Trusts: The Backbone

For real control, you build a revocable living trust. This trust lets you move assets—house, bank accounts, investments—under the trust's name while you're still here. You stay in charge as trustee. If something happens, a backup you chose steps in—no court waiting period. They follow clear instructions you left in the trust papers.

This tool is made for parents of kids who aren't adults yet. You spell out exactly how money can be used: tuition, braces, summer sports, help with college someday. You decide if the trust gives lump sums at certain ages or only pays for essentials till a milestone. No probate means kids' guardian or trustee gets access to funds immediately—with no judge in the way. The law walks you through the details, and a good attorney makes sure every piece fits. It's reliable—and fast when it matters.

Beneficiary Designations and Pay-on-Death (POD) Accounts

You don't always need a big trust. Some accounts and policies let you pick a beneficiary—life insurance, IRAs, bank accounts, employer plans. These pass straight to the named person after death. But there's a trap: naming a minor as a beneficiary doesn't work. Banks won't hand assets to anyone under 18. Money stalls or ends up in the court's hands.

Instead, name your revocable living trust (or a trusted adult) as beneficiary. That way, someone you picked manages every dollar the way you intended, without detours through conservatorship. Make sure your beneficiary forms match the rest of your plan. Details here matter.

Beneficiary Deeds and Joint Ownership

Real estate moves with a signature. You can record a "beneficiary deed." On paper, it's a transfer-on-death deed. You keep owning the house during your life. When you pass, the deed instantly flips title to whoever you named—or to your trust if you're thinking ahead. No court, no waiting, nobody second-guessing you. For minor kids, making the trust the beneficiary avoids snags with kids holding title before they're adults.

Owning your house "joint tenancy with right of survivorship" between spouses is another route. When one dies, the other takes full ownership, simple as that. Don't put a child on the title as a joint owner—they legally can't hold real estate, and you risk complications, liens, even loss of property.

Picking the People to Guard and Guide Your Kids

Nothing in this process ranks higher than naming a guardian for your kids. The law lets you do it in your will. When both parents are gone or can't provide care, the guardian steps in for everyday life—school pickups, doctor visits, steadying the house. The judge has final approval. In most cases, they respect your choice unless strong evidence says otherwise.

Property for minors demands a separate steward. The trustee holds the purse strings if you set up a trust; a conservator runs point if it's through the courts. It can be one person or two: maybe your sister who's great with kids, and your brother-in-law who's sharp with numbers. What matters is spelling out responsibilities. Be clear. Lay out guidance for spending on health, school, support, and growing up. If you don't, stranger hands might manage everything you leave.

Probate without guidance means uncertainty. It means your kids' future gets decided by someone who wasn't at your dinner table. Making firm choices now gives your children familiar faces and predictable support, money and care coming from people who know them best.

Extra Layers for Real Life

Plans Change—So Should Your Documents

Life doesn't sit still. Another child is born, incomes shift, relationships change. Good estate planning isn't "set it and forget it." Review your papers and accounts every few years or after big turning points. Make sure trust terms, beneficiary forms, and guardian picks still fit. Small details can come back to haunt you if left out of date.

What Happens if You're Still Alive, But Can't Decide?

Don't forget the risk of incapacity—car wreck, illness, anything that takes your judgment away. Most states let you create durable powers of attorney for finances and healthcare. With those, the person you name pays bills, handles the hospital, and stands in for critical choices. Nothing needs a judge's say-so. These forms fill a gap that too many families leave to chance.

Telling the Right People the Right Things

No plan works if the players are in the dark. Don't just file papers and cross your fingers. Tell your chosen guardians and trustees what you expect of them. Share the location of your documents and discuss the "why" behind choices, at least in broad strokes. If you want, write a letter of wishes—lay out your hopes, not just your instructions. It keeps tempers cool and reduces arguments when emotions run high.

Staying Ready—Execution and Upkeep

You can have the perfect estate plan on paper—and still fail your family if the details aren't buttoned down. Make sure every account, deed, and insurance policy is in order and points to the right trust, person, or beneficiary. Keep originals or copies in a locked but findable spot. Tell family or key advisors where to look if disaster comes.

You don't have to go it alone. Estate planning attorneys know the mechanics and can catch mistakes before they get expensive. Procedures, signatures, and state-specific quirks matter. Set a reminder to check up on your plan every year or after a major life shift. What works for a family of three can miss the mark for a family of five.

This is the backbone work parents do for love, not just legality. A well-built estate plan lets your children keep living—secure, grounded, cared for—no matter what storms come. It's not about riches. It's about readiness. When you've done the work, your family won't be caught waiting on the courthouse. That peace—knowing they're protected—is the lasting result.

SECTION 4: GUARDIANSHIP FOR MINOR CHILDREN

NAMING A GUARDIAN: THE LEGAL GAPS YOU'LL WISH YOU'D CLOSED

You can see the question plain as day—who steps in for your child if you're suddenly not here? For parents, naming a guardian is not just a tough emotional call. It's a binding legal act, and if you get it wrong or skip a step, it can haunt your family later. I've seen too many parents believe their intentions were clear, only to watch the courts unravel everything. It starts with good intentions, ends with regrets. Courts don't care how close you were or who "always promised." They follow signed papers, not stories.

The Big Missteps When Picking a Guardian

It's easy to assume everyone's on the same page, but simple talk or leaving instructions stashed in a drawer is how chaos starts. Most disasters happen slowly, then all at once, when families realize nobody nailed down the details.

1. Depending on Verbal Promises or Informal Notes

You can tell your best friend he's the guy. You can even write it out in an email or leave a scribbled letter in a file. None of that holds water in court. If disaster strikes and there's no will on file—nothing executed properly—your wishes get wiped off the table. The probate judge makes the call. They'll listen, sometimes, but your email or letter is just background noise. Only a clear, signed will or, in rare cases, a statutory declaration, can make your choice stick. Everything else is wishful thinking.

2. Naming a Single Guardian and Skipping an Alternate

Life is unpredictable. Maybe your sister, the planned guardian, moves across the country or has a health crisis. I've watched courts scramble for a backup when the only nomination bows out. If you didn't list an alternate—or rotate your picks as years go by—a complete stranger may end up with your kid. It's that simple. Always choose at least one backup. Even better, make time every few years to see if your picks still make sense. Families change, so does life.

3. Not Checking Legal and Practical Suitability

Your favorite cousin might be good with kids, but is he over 18? Is he healthy, stable, and reliable enough to step up? The law is blunt here: no adults under 18, nobody of unsound mind, and anyone the court considers "unsuitable" is off the table—no matter what your will says. If you nominate someone out of state, expect more paperwork, more delays, maybe more expense. I've seen people name someone far away, only to tie the court in knots. Take a hard look at your nominee's real ability and location. Don't leave the court guessing.

4. Failing to Warn or Consult the Guardian

If you don't ask the person you want to be guardian—or at least tell them clearly—you're gambling. It's happened plenty: someone opens the will and gets blindsided by the news they're on the hook for a child. Some refuse, some accept and then collapse under the weight. Your child deserves better than crossed wires. Have the talk, awkward or not. Get a clear "yes." Make sure your guardian knows the stakes and is willing to serve. Skip this step and you may leave the decision in strangers' hands.

5. Vague or Unworkable Instructions

I've read wills that said, "If Mark and Sue can't do it, their best friend will," or tied guardianship to conditions like "so long as they live in our old house." Courts toss out what they can't enforce. If you pick a couple, and they separate, who takes over? Unclear directions lead to confusion and sometimes to lawsuits. Get candid with instructions and spell out what you want in simple, enforceable language. Talk through messy scenarios while there's still time.

6. Forgetting to Split the Jobs: Guardian vs. Trustee

The best guardian isn't always a master with money. You can name one person to care for the child, another to oversee inheritance or property. That line matters. If you name only a guardian and hand them all your assets too, you risk financial conflict or mismanagement—especially if that person struggles with numbers. Setting up a trust, picking a responsible trustee, and spelling out limits protects both your child and their future. One person can do both jobs—if they're up to it. Most families fare better keeping duty and dollars separate.

7. Letting Years Pass Without Updating Your Will

Families fracture, people move, health fades. The aunt you trusted at age three might not fit when your child is fifteen. Divorce or a falling out can flip old choices on their head. The most common regret comes from never stopping to look at old documents until crisis hits. Build a habit: every few years, or after a major life change, check your will. Confirm your choices still stand.

What Courts Do When the Paperwork Fails

When there is no signed will, or the names no longer fit reality, courts step in. The judge doesn't know your stories—they follow the law and look for the "best interest of the child." If there's a legal nomination in your will, they'll start there. If not, they sort through relatives, weigh petitions, and sometimes spark years of family battles before picking anyone. I've seen children caught in the crossfire while adults argue over them in court. The process drags on—delays are standard, not rare—especially when feuding relatives enter the mix or challenge your choices.

If both parents die or become incapable, and no sound legal document exists, the court may send the child to temporary foster care until they can sort it out. Some older children are asked their preference, but the law decides, not their wishes. Skip the paperwork, and you gamble with the outcome. Some kids end up bounced from one adult to another, never landing where their parents hoped.

Tougher Cases: Blended Families and Strained Relationships

Blended families are common, but the law still works from bloodlines. Step-parents don't get guardian status unless there's a legal adoption. If you don't name names in your will, estranged siblings or distant cousins might file their own claims. I've watched families tied up for years over an unclear plan. If yours is complicated, spell out every intention. Do not assume the judge "will know what you mean."

How to Lock In Your Wishes—and Avoid the Usual Regrets

The fixes aren't hard but demand full attention. I've seen too many families trust fate and luck. Here is what actually works on the ground.

Write a Clear Will the Court Can Enforce

There's no shortcut—your wishes only count if they're in a valid will. Work with a lawyer who knows their stuff when it comes to the rules. Handwritten notes, phone calls, or casual letters won't protect your family. Sign your name the right way, file it, and keep it where someone can find it.

Pick Backups. Revisit Every Few Years.

Always list a backup guardian, sometimes a second. Situations shift: job loss, death, new family drama. Set a calendar reminder every couple of years, or trigger a review with big life changes: divorce, marriage, relocation, anything that matters. A stale list means rolling the dice on the judge's mercy.

Be Direct—And Honest—About Who's Truly Able

Use legal names, provide up-to-date contact info. If you're naming a couple, explain what should happen if they split up or can't both serve. Spell out basic hopes for your child's upbringing, but ditch "only if" demands the court can't enforce. Measure your guardian's limits—their finances, their family life, connection to your child. Don't just chase your ideals. Pick reality over wishful thinking.

Keep Money and Parenting Roles Separate When It Helps

Most kids are better off if you divide the weight between two people: a guardian for care, a trustee for money. That way, nobody's overloaded and there's less room for trouble. A lawyer can help you set up a trust or clear plan for how the money should be used, what counts as necessity, and how education or support gets paid out.

Loop in Everyone Who Matters

Don't make this a secret kept to the grave. Bring the named guardian into the conversation. Ask alternates to step up as well. Let family members know what's coming, and tell your lawyer why you picked the people you did. If you suspect infighting, keep notes on your reasons. Clear, honest conversations now keep your wishes from unraveling when no one can ask you what you meant.

If Your Family's Complicated, Put Everything in Writing

Blended families, ex-spouses, estranged kin—don't trust the system to figure them out for you. Spell out relationships, intentions, and the logic behind your choices. Let your lawyer review the words, so nothing gets lost in translation or buried by ambiguous phrasing.

Parents—Don't Leave This to Chance

One piece of paper, done right, can spare your child years of uncertainty and legal wrangling. Keep your documents current. Talk to your people. Nail down every name and plan you want to stand. Courts follow the letter—not the story—so make your letter clear. It's work nobody wants to do, but silence leaves too much room for mistakes.

UNDERSTANDING GUARDIANSHIP

Guardianship is a legal process where a probate court appoints a person or entity (the guardian) to make personal decisions for an individual (the ward) who has been deemed incapacitated. This ensures the ward's safety and well-being when they can no longer manage their own affairs.

Nobody wants to talk about losing control. But sometimes, life throws a curveball. An accident. A sudden illness. The slow march of dementia. When someone can no longer make safe decisions for themselves, for their health, or for their daily life, the state has a process in place to help: Guardianship. This isn't about taking away freedom arbitrarily. It's about providing a necessary safety net for those who can no longer advocate for themselves. Understanding how this system works, is critical for families.

What is Guardianship? And How Does It Differ from Conservatorship?

People often use "guardianship" as a catch-all term. It's more specific. A guardian is appointed by a probate court to make personal decisions for an incapacitated person. This includes things like medical care, living arrangements, education, and social activities. The court calls the person under guardianship a "ward."

Then there's conservatorship. A conservator is appointed to manage the financial affairs of someone deemed "disabled." This means handling assets, paying bills, making investments, and protecting their estate. Often, the same person or entity serves as both guardian and conservator for an individual. But they are distinct legal roles with separate responsibilities and court oversight. The distinction is important, even if the same person fills both shoes. It means two separate sets of duties, two separate sets of accountings to the court. It's not a small job.

Who Needs a Guardian?

A guardian is appointed for an individual, called an "incapacitated person," who can no longer make or communicate decisions about their own care, custody, or well-being. This inability must be due to a mental or physical condition. It's not about simply making bad decisions; it's about being unable to make decisions at all. The court makes this determination based on evidence, not just someone's opinion.

Common scenarios include:

- Elderly individuals with advanced dementia or Alzheimer's.
- Adults with severe developmental disabilities.
- Individuals who have suffered a traumatic brain injury or stroke and cannot manage their personal needs.
- Minors whose parents are deceased or unfit, and no other suitable arrangement exists.

The standard is high. The court looks for "clear and convincing evidence" of incapacitation. This protects the individual's rights. It's their life, after all.

The Legal Process: Petition to Appointment

The Guardianship process starts with a petition filed in the probate court. Anyone with an interest in the alleged incapacitated person's welfare can file this petition. Often, it's a family member, a social worker, or a concerned friend.

Here's a general rundown of what happens:

- Filing the Petition:
  The petitioner asks the court to declare someone incapacitated and appoint a guardian (and possibly a conservator). They need to provide reasons and evidence.
- Notice:
  The alleged incapacitated person and their close relatives must receive formal notice of the petition. This is a fundamental due process right. They have the right to object.
- Guardian Ad Litem:
  The court typically appoints an attorney, a "guardian ad litem," to represent the best interests of the alleged incapacitated person. This lawyer's job is to investigate, meet with the person, and report back to the court. They are a crucial check in the system.
- Medical Examination:
  The court will usually require a medical or psychological evaluation to assess the person's capacity. This provides objective evidence.
- Hearing:
  A formal hearing takes place. The judge hears testimony, reviews evidence, and listens to the guardian ad litem's report. The alleged incapacitated person has the right to be present and represented by their own attorney.
- Court Order:
  If the court finds clear and convincing evidence of incapacitation, it will issue an order appointing a guardian and/or conservator. The order specifies the guardian's powers and duties.

This process can be complex and emotionally taxing. Having experienced legal counsel is essential.

Responsibilities of a Guardian

Being a guardian is a serious responsibility. It's not a title; it's a job. A guardian must act in the best interests of their ward. This includes:

- Personal Care:
  Making decisions about medical treatment, personal hygiene, food, clothing, and shelter.
- Living Arrangements:
  Deciding where the ward will live, whether it's at home, with family, or in a care facility.
- Social and Recreational Activities:
  Ensuring the ward has opportunities for social interaction and engaging activities.
- Education:
  If the ward is a minor or an adult with special educational needs, the guardian oversees their schooling.
- Reporting to the Court:
  Guardians must file annual reports with the probate court, detailing the ward's condition, living situation, and any significant decisions made. This ensures accountability.

The court maintains oversight. If a guardian fails in their duties, they can be removed. It's a system designed to protect the vulnerable.

Limited Guardianship vs. Full Guardianship

The law prefers to grant the least restrictive form of guardianship possible. This means if an individual can still make some decisions, the court will try to limit the guardian's power to only those areas where help is truly needed. This is called "limited guardianship."

For example, a person might be able to decide where they want to live but struggle with complex medical decisions. A limited guardian might only be appointed for healthcare matters. A "full" or "general" guardianship, where the guardian makes all personal decisions, is reserved for cases of total incapacitation.

The goal is always to maximize the ward's autonomy while ensuring their safety. It's a delicate balance, and the court takes it seriously.

Alternatives to Guardianship

Guardianship should always be a last resort. Proactive estate planning can often prevent the need for court intervention. Key documents include:

- Durable Power of Attorney for Healthcare:
  This document allows you to name an agent to make medical decisions for you if you become incapacitated. It avoids the need for a guardian of the person.
- Durable Power of Attorney for Finances:
  This allows you to name an agent to manage your financial affairs. It avoids the need for a conservator.
- Trusts:
  A well-drafted trust can manage assets for your benefit if you become incapacitated, again bypassing the need for a conservator.

These documents give you control. You choose who makes decisions for you, and under what circumstances. Without them, the court steps in, and a judge makes those choices for you. It's a powerful reason to plan ahead, while you still can. Learn more about how a Power of Attorney
can provide peace of mind.

Facing a Guardianship?

Whether you're considering petitioning for Guardianship for a loved one, or you're an alleged incapacitated person facing a petition, the legal process can feel overwhelming. The stakes are high: personal autonomy, financial stability, and family harmony. Working with an attorney familiar with probate courts and guardianship law is essential. We understand the nuances of these cases and can guide you through every step, protecting your rights and advocating for the best possible outcome.

Understanding Guardianship is not just about legal terms; it's about protecting dignity and ensuring care for those who need it most. Plan wisely, act thoughtfully.

IF YOU DON'T PLAN: WHAT HAPPENS TO YOUR CHILDREN

Parenthood—and the Things Most People Don't Talk About

When you bring a child home—tiny fingers gripping yours—you think about car seats, diapers, sleep. You don't think about what happens if you're not there. Most don't. New parents often skip over estate planning, figuring it's for retired couples or families with vacation homes. That's not how it works. If anything, the need runs deeper for parents with young children still in the house.

Who do you trust with everything if you and your spouse can't be there? If you die or become unable to parent, the state steps in with its own process. In most states, that means slow courts, paperwork, and strangers making choices that should have been yours. The chance to protect your child from instability—or even a courtroom fight—begins long before disaster. If you get it down in a plan, your wishes control what comes next.

What The Law Actually Does If You Leave It To Chance

Here's where the shoe drops. If you haven't written down your directions and both parents are gone or out of commission, the courts take over. No one gets to just pick up your child and head home. The law forces things to play out in a specific order. Relatives may hope to step in fast, but it starts—and sometimes stalls—in probate court. The gears of government do not turn quickly for orphans.

Guardianship: Who Calls the Shots For Your Child

Guardianship isn't just "who takes them home." It's a legal designation—a person who is authorized to make decisions for your underage child about where they live, how they're raised, and even what medical treatment they get. If you named someone as guardian in a valid will, the court takes your word. If not, anyone—usually blood relatives—can petition for the job, and the judge holds hearings, often in front of a wary child. Many states give parents the right to choose, but only if you do it in writing. No nomination? The judge sorts it out. Sometimes that means pitting family against family. The court rules in "the best interest of the child," but it's a cold process, and it can end with your child in a home you never pictured for them.

Depending on how things go, the role might go to a public guardian or someone barely known to your child. Family fights happen. Sometimes both sides leave disappointed. That's how the law is written. If the person you trust isn't on paper, it's out of your hands.

Who Manages The Money? (And Why It's Rarely Simple)

If you leave no will or trust, the state uses intestacy laws to split up assets. Your children inherit. Sounds direct, but children can't handle money—not legally or practically—so the court appoints a conservator. This could be a different person from the guardian—sometimes it's a cousin, sometimes a stranger, occasionally even an attorney. That means one person decides how your child spends each day, and another holds the checkbook.

The conservator faces paperwork just to make routine purchases. They have to post a bond and file annual reports with the court, which drags in costs and delays. If the guardianship and conservatorship don't line up, squabbles and logjams follow. When your child turns 18, the conservatorship vanishes and any remaining funds are handed over all at once, whether your kid is prudent or not. If your plan was "they'll figure it out," remember: 18 is young. The system doesn't care. No flexibility, no guardrails, and money can slip through their fingers without guidance.

If You Take The Reins: What Real Planning Looks Like

If you want a say in your child's future, it has to be in writing. Estate planning isn't just about assets; it's about where your child wakes up, who tucks them in, who decides if a surgery happens. If you care about any of these details, you need a plan.

Name a Guardian That Means Something to You

The clearest step is naming a guardian in a will—signed, witnessed, no shortcuts. List your first choice, then a backup. These aren't academic decisions. It's looking at your real life and the people in it. If the court sees your nomination and there's no evidence of unfitness, it goes through. Put it down on paper, sign it, and you've just cut down on doubt, courtroom wrangling, and family drama when your child needs stability most.

Setting Up a Trust For Your Kids—And Why It Matters

Most parents look at their house and life insurance, nod, and walk away. But leaving money outright to your minor children isn't good practice. Establishing a trust—either inside your will or as an outside document—means you decide when your child gets access, who manages the spending, and for what purpose. You can keep the money out of their hands at 18, if that's what makes sense. Education, living expenses, health—handled as you intended. It's run by a trustee you choose, not just someone the system lands on. Trusts cut through red tape, side-step court conservatorships, and offer flexibility you won't get from the state's default plan. You can even stagger inheritance for milestones—whatever fits what you know of your child.

Don't Just Think Long-Term—Plan For Emergencies Too

Life doesn't always collapse in the ways we expect. Sometimes you're in the hospital or stuck overseas. Most states support short-term powers of attorney for minors, letting you pick someone trusted to make medical, educational, or even day-to-day decisions while you're gone. It's paperwork, but it's the easiest way to keep your child from getting lost in a moment of chaos. Get it set up, keep it with your estate papers.

This Isn't Easy—But You Have to Pick Someone

No candidate is perfect. People move, families change, and sometimes willingness shifts. Evaluate by real character, their location, their health, and their actual willingness to do the work. Talk to them—don't make assumptions. The law lets you list alternates if your top pick can't serve. Revisit these choices as the years go by. A plan that worked when your child was two may not work at sixteen.

Life: What Else Parents Should Consider

Life Insurance Is Usually Your Biggest Asset

Don't underestimate your policy. For plenty of parents, life insurance is the largest source of cash a child might ever see. Do not set your minor child as the direct beneficiary. If you do, courts may freeze the money or lock it into conservatorships, with all their hoops and costs. Name a trust as the beneficiary, and you keep the money working for your child without extra court hands on the lever.

Be Careful With Beneficiary Choices

Banks, retirement accounts, "payable-on-death" forms: these move assets without respect for your will. Review every few years. Never leave anything direct to a minor if you can help it. Complexity comes fast when beneficiary forms and your will don't line up.

If Your Child Has Special Needs

If your child relies on government benefits—think Medicaid

or SSI—a simple inheritance can do more harm than good. Most states allows supplemental needs trusts, set up to hold gifts for your disabled child without killing their eligibility for help. It's a specialty, but if it applies, ask for it. The long-term security at stake is real.

A Plan Is the Best Gift You Can Give

No one likes thinking about worst-case scenarios, but most parents would do nearly anything to make life easier for their kids. Estate planning isn't fear-mongering—it's taking care of business so your children get care, stability, and guidance if you can't be there. It hands you the tools to choose your child's guardian, safeguard their inheritance, and keep family from fighting at the worst possible time.

If you leave these decisions to the courts, you're gambling with your family's future. But with a will, a trust, and a little legwork now, you keep control. It's one of the few ways to offer real protection for your family—when words and wishes alone are no longer enough.

WHY ESTATE PLANNING CAN'T WAIT UNTIL KIDS ARE OLDER

Turning 18: The Door Closes Quietly

The reality hits fast. Your child turns eighteen, and the world quietly swaps the locks. The law marks the passage with a clean break—one day you're making doctor appointments for them, settling tuition, talking with teachers. The next, those doors are barred. The law recognizes your young adult—emphasis on adult—and shuts parents out of nearly every decision by default.

The rituals of adulthood get all the attention. Diplomas, dorm room shopping, car keys. But nobody sets off fireworks for the phone call where a clinic says, politely but firmly, that Mom no longer has access. Life moves fast. HIPAA backs it up. No records, no decisions, no bank instructions—unless the right documents are in place. It doesn't matter how involved you've been.

Parents put off estate planning, thinking it's a matter for midlife. That fiction tempts everyone. But the tools—powers of attorney and HIPAA forms—aren't about inheritances or preparing for the end. They're about making sure someone can act quickly if your 18-year-old is hurt, distant, or just out of commission. A few signatures can head off a world of heartache. It's about control in a crisis, not paperwork for retirement.

What Every 18-Year-Old Needs Signed—Now

A good estate plan for someone fresh out of high school isn't complicated, but it matters. Life can turn on a dime. These documents aren't about money—they're about sidestepping legal brick walls in a bad moment. No one expects their healthy kid to end up unreachable. It happens.

Durable Power of Attorney for Healthcare

This isn't a formality. We talked about it before. Better to talk about those choices now, not during an emergency.

HIPAA Authorization

Hospital staff work behind locked doors. Without HIPAA Authorizaiton, you won't even get a status update—no matter how frantic the call.

Durable Financial Power of Attorney

Money doesn't pause for emergencies. Bank accounts, bills, student loans—if something happens, the bills still come due. A missed flight, hospitalization, or gap year abroad can lock a young person out of their own finances and leave parents unable to help.

Will or Beneficiary Designations

A will at this age isn't about wealth. It marks responsibility.

How Families Can Get Things Done

It isn't rocket science to get this right. Sit down, talk about the future, then figure out who gets the call if something happens. Don't wait for a scare. Gather a list of important accounts—anything with money or insurance attached—because many need updated beneficiaries once the kid turns eighteen. The hardest part is scheduling the honest talk.

Find a lawyer who does this often. They'll help you decide what goes in or stays out. It's usually one consultation, maybe an hour—signed, notarized, state-compliant. The cost barely registers compared to a tangled emergency.

Review papers again every couple of years. Nobody's life stands still at eighteen.

This Is About Control—Not Surrender

Estate planning, at its core, arms young adults and their families against chaos. Signing these forms is not surrender. It's a test of readiness—one that clears a path for the family to help if the call comes in from a hospital or bank.

Parents who get ahead of this don't do it out of paranoia. They do it to remove barriers when life spins sideways. With the right documents, their support lands as intended, no court orders or last-minute scrambling.

Young or old, wealthy or scraping by—it doesn't matter. This is the work of stepping into adulthood and staying ready for whatever shows up on the road ahead.

SECTION 5: MEDICAID & LONG-TERM CARE PLANNING

STATE OF MISSOURI MEDICAID OFFICE

This section is based on Missouri. Every state will have its own system that will be somewhat similar and somewhat different. This will help guide non-Missourians but they will need to verify their state's information.

The State Of Missouri Medicaid Office refers to the various divisions and agencies within the Missouri Department of Social Services (DSS) responsible for administering MO HealthNet, the state's Medicaid program. This office manages applications, determines eligibility for medical assistance, and oversees benefits for low-income individuals, families, and those needing long-term care across Missouri.

Navigating government services is rarely straightforward. The State Of Missouri Medicaid Office is no exception. It's a critical resource for many Missourians, especially when long-term care becomes a reality. But understanding how it works, what it covers, and who qualifies? That's where things get complicated. We're going to break it down. You need to know this stuff.

What is Missouri Medicaid (MO HealthNet)?

First, let's get the name right. In Missouri, Medicaid is called MO HealthNet. It's a federal and state program. It provides healthcare coverage. This includes doctor visits, hospital stays, prescription drugs, and, significantly, long-term care services for eligible low-income individuals. Eligibility varies. It depends on age, income, family size, pregnancy status, disability, and medical need. MO HealthNet is not a one-size-fits-all program. There are different categories, each with its own rules. This complexity often catches people off guard. Don't assume you know the rules without checking. They change. The official portal for the program is MO HealthNet Division. It's a good place to start for general program information, but it won't detail specific planning strategies.

Understanding the Application Process

Applying for MO HealthNet means dealing with the State Of Missouri Medicaid Office, specifically the Family Support Division (FSD) of the Department of Social Services. It's not a quick phone call. The application process is thorough. You'll need to provide extensive documentation. We're talking birth certificates, social security cards, proof of income, bank statements, asset records, and more. Missing paperwork or errors can cause significant delays. Or outright denial. You can apply online, by mail, or in person at a local FSD office. Be prepared. It's a bureaucracy, and it runs on paper and patience. Don't rush it. Get it right the first time.

Local offices are your direct point of contact for submitting forms and asking questions about your specific application. They are the frontline of the State Of Missouri Medicaid Office. Don't underestimate the value of a complete, accurate application. It saves time and stress down the road. The federal government also provides resources and guidance on state programs through agencies like the U.S. Department of Health & Human Services, which offers an overarching view.

Eligibility Requirements: Income, Assets, and the Look-Back Period

This is where estate planning and Medicaid intersect directly. MO HealthNet eligibility involves strict income and asset limits. These limits are specific and change regularly. For many, especially those needing long-term care, their assets exceed these limits. This doesn't mean you're out of luck. It means you need a plan. The "look-back period" is critical here. Currently, for long-term care Medicaid, Missouri has a 60-month (five-year) look-back period. What does this mean? The State Of Missouri Medicaid Office will review all financial transactions made by the applicant during the 60 months prior to their application date. Any uncompensated transfers – gifts, selling assets for less than fair market value – can trigger a penalty period. During this penalty period, Medicaid won't pay for care. This is a major trap for the unprepared. You can't just give away your assets right before you apply. The government sees that coming a mile away.

Understanding these asset rules is non-negotiable for proper estate planning. Certain assets are "exempt" or "non-countable," like your primary residence (up to a certain equity limit), one vehicle, and personal belongings. But most other assets, including bank accounts, investments, and second properties, are countable. This is why proactive planning is essential. Waiting until a crisis hits often leaves fewer options and more expensive solutions.

Missouri Revised Statutes Chapter 208 outlines many of these eligibility criteria. Check it. Understand it. The equity limit for a home, for instance, is a common point of confusion. It can be a significant amount, but it's not unlimited. This is where the details matter, and overlooking them can cost you.

The Role of the Family Support Division (FSD)

When we talk about the State Of Missouri Medicaid Office, we are primarily referring to the Family Support Division (FSD) within the Missouri Department of Social Services (DSS). The FSD handles all applications for MO HealthNet. They determine eligibility. They process renewals. They are the gatekeepers. Their staff reviews your financial records, medical needs, and personal situation against the state's complex rules. They also manage other programs, like SNAP and Temporary Assistance. Their job is to ensure you meet every single requirement. No exceptions. They operate under federal and state guidelines. It's a system. You need to know how to work within it.

You can find more information about the FSD and their services on the official Missouri Department of Social Services website. This site provides forms, office locations, and general program details. It's a good starting point, but it won't replace tailored legal advice. Remember, the FSD agents are there to process applications according to the law. They aren't there to give you advice on how to legally qualify. That's a critical distinction.

Long-Term Care and Medicaid Planning

This is where proactive legal work pays off. Many people don't think about Medicaid until they or a loved one needs nursing home care. The cost of long-term care in Missouri is staggering. It can quickly wipe out a lifetime of savings. MO HealthNet is often the only way to cover these costs without bankrupting a family. Effective Medicaid planning involves legally restructuring assets. This must be done well in advance of needing care. It's about protecting your legacy while ensuring you qualify for necessary assistance. Strategies might include using certain trusts, making permissible transfers, or converting countable assets into non-countable ones. For example, a properly structured irrevocable trust can protect assets from being counted towards Medicaid eligibility after the look-back period expires. This is complex stuff. It requires an attorney with specific expertise in Missouri Medicaid law. Don't try this alone. The stakes are too high. The federal Medicaid website also provides general information on long-term services and supports, but state rules are paramount.

One powerful tool in this planning is a durable power of attorney. This document allows a trusted agent to manage your financial affairs, including executing Medicaid planning strategies, if you become incapacitated. Without one, a guardianship might be necessary, adding cost and complexity. You want control. A POA gives you that. It's not just for end-of-life. It's for managing your affairs when you can't. Make sure your POA specifically grants the necessary powers for Medicaid planning. A generic POA might not cut it. This is a common oversight. Without these specific powers, your agent might be legally unable to implement critical Medicaid planning steps, even if they know what needs to be done. This is a setup for failure.

Appeals and Denials

What if your MO HealthNet application is denied? Don't panic. But don't give up either. You have the right to appeal. The denial letter from the State Of Missouri Medicaid Office will explain why your application was denied and how to request a fair hearing. This is your opportunity to present additional information or argue why the decision was incorrect. Appeals have strict deadlines, usually 90 days from the date of the notice. Miss the deadline, and you lose your chance. This is another area where legal counsel is invaluable. An attorney can review the denial, identify the issues, gather evidence, and represent you at the hearing. It's a formal process, much like a court case. Treat it as such. The IM-80 form is often used for appeals in Missouri, initiating the fair hearing process. Getting professional help at this stage can significantly improve your chances of a successful outcome. Don't go into a hearing unprepared against a state agency.

Local Assistance in Missouri

While the rules are statewide, local FSD offices can provide direct assistance with applications. However, their role is administrative. They cannot provide legal advice or complex planning strategies. For that, you need an experienced estate planning attorney. An attorney who understands the nuances of Missouri Medicaid law can help you navigate the eligibility rules, protect your assets, and ensure your application is as strong as possible. Don't go it alone. The system is designed to be challenging. Get professional help. It's a smart investment. We've seen too many families lose significant assets because they tried to figure it out themselves or relied on well-meaning but unqualified advice.

The State Of Missouri Medicaid Office, primarily through the Family Support Division, plays a pivotal role in providing essential healthcare coverage. Especially for long-term care. Navigating its rules and requirements is complex. It involves strict income and asset limits, a five-year look-back period, and a demanding application process. Proactive planning is key to protecting your assets and securing eligibility. Don't wait for a crisis to understand MO HealthNet. Understand it now. Plan now. It makes all the difference. Your peace of mind and financial security depend on it.

HOW TO SHIELD YOUR HOME FROM NURSING HOME SPEND-DOWN

The old brick house on the corner, the porch swing, acres you mowed every weekend—that's more than real estate. For most families, the house is what ties blood and memory to the ground. But when a parent or spouse faces nursing home care, that same home can slip into jeopardy faster than folks expect. Under Medicaid's spend-down rules, the house can become a pawn on the way to a government claim. Knowing how those rules work—before the health crisis hits—lets you push back and keep the place in the family.

The Mechanics Nursing Home Spend-Down Rules

You write the first check to the nursing facility. Next month, another. The cost racks up into the thousands. Most families run out of savings and turn to Medicaid, a program with sharp eligibility lines. As of 2024, a single person can keep just $5,726 in "countable assets." Anything above that needs to get spent down or reclassified before Medicaid steps in.

Not everything is thrown on the table. At first glance, Medicaid labels the main house "exempt". It doesn't count against the applicant—right away. The catch is, nothing about these rules is simple or permanent. Without groundwork, your home stays exposed, either to claims from the state after death or if the living situation twists again. The exemption is a shield, but it's made of glass. Understand how and when it breaks.

When Does the Home Stay Off-Limits?

Here's the baseline: as long as the house is the Medicaid applicant's "principal place of residence," and equity is under $713,000 (in 2024), it stays off the Medicaid asset list. If a spouse, dependent child, or certain relatives live there, the exemption usually holds up while Medicaid pays the nursing home. Different story if the resident is single and won't return home, or the house sells the "wrong" way. That's when the protection falls through a crack.

Even if the house stays protected while you're alive, death changes the equation. State Estate Recovery Programs let the state demand repayment for every Medicaid dollar spent. The most common way: lay claim to the house or other estate assets during probate. Without planning, your kids may get a lawyer's letter instead of house keys.

How People Actually Protect Their House

No single fix. It comes down to legal paperwork, timing, and family dynamics. Each move has trade-offs. If you want to keep the old place out of probate or from being scooped up by the state, you need to weigh all options—preferably with a sharp estate lawyer who's done this a hundred times.

1. Life Estate Deed: Giving Up, But Not Going Away

With a life estate deed, you sign over your house to the next generation (mainly kids), but reserve the right to live in it until you die. This often slips the property past probate and out of reach of Medicaid's estate claim. The legal interest moves out of your name, but you keep the right to stay put as long as you're living.

Before you sign, know what you're giving up. You can't sell the place or refinance without their say-so. Family ties get complicated. Plus, if you do this inside the five-year Medicaid "look-back," you hit a penalty phase—potentially losing coverage until money runs out. Good news is the state typically won't get the house if done early enough. The catch? Taxes and messy family dynamics. They don't put that in the brochures.

2. Irrevocable Trust: Out of Reach, But Out of Your Hands

Put the house in an irrevocable trust—one drafted for Medicaid rules—and you're no longer the legal owner, the trust is. That's good news. So long as you don't have control or access to revoke it, and do it more than five years before applying, Medicaid sees the house as belonging to your beneficiaries, not you. The state can't claw it back after death.

But you can't back out or take it with you. This isn't for people who change their minds every five years. You lose power over the home. To get it right, the trust needs precise legal drafting—there's no "undo" button if you mess up. This is a long game. Most families who win started early.

3. Spouse or Disabled Child Remains: The Short-Term Shield

If a spouse or protected disabled child still lives in the home, Medicaid rules say leave it alone. The state won't force a sale or count it against eligibility. As long as the spouse breathes under that roof, the house is off-limits. Once both are gone, the shield drops unless you've arranged a new transfer to keep the house out of probate or state hands.

The shelter lasts as long as a spouse or protected child lives there. For anyone else, default rules kick back in, and you'll want that next planning step—a deed or trust—to keep the state from swooping in after funerals are over.

4. Transfer-On-Death Deed: The Shortcut

Most states lets you file a "beneficiary deed." This legal move puts your house on autopilot when you pass—straight to named heirs without court or probate. Real advantage: assets that never land in probate usually skip the Medicaid estate recovery claim.

The paperwork must be tight. File and record it right with the county, ahead of death, following every technical step or it won't work. Don't try to skirt the rules mid-life—giving away the house while you're living (instead of at death) can spark Medicaid penalties if inside that five-year window.

5. The Five-Year Look-Back: Hidden Trap, Hard Deadline

Everything hangs on the Medicaid look-back. Transfers for less than fair market value, including gifts to family, trigger a long penalty if made inside five years before you file. They don't care if you needed the money or wanted to reward a loyal child. Value exchanged for time, that's the rule. Penalty equals the value of what was transferred, divided by monthly care costs. It's a clean calculation, brutal in effect.

Wait too long and options shrink. Moves executed before that five-year bell avoid penalty. After, you're exposed. Early action isn't just useful—it's the only safe play.

The Value of Acting While You Still Can

Waiting until your health is failing almost always costs more. Locks on the doors and old photos on the wall can't replace real planning. The people who keep their homes are usually the ones who worked with advisors, signed the right deed or trust, and did it long before the doctors said "long-term care."

No quick fix. The law changes. One family's fix is another's disaster. Exemptions for spouses and kids, custom trusts, setting up transfer-on-death paperwork—each works only if tailored. Don't fall for shortcuts. A good lawyer does more than paperwork. They help keep the house where it belongs long after you're gone.

If you want to pass along a legacy instead of a legal mess, map it out while there's time. Every empty house is a story that ended one step short. Don't let the state write the last line for you.

MEDICAID PLANNING VS. ESTATE PLANNING: WHAT ACTUALLY MATTERS

Sit down with a family sorting out their future, and two words come up: Medicaid, estate. One pulls toward protecting assets in case long-term care wipes you out. The other tries to lock in some certainty—who gets what, who makes the call if you can't. They overlap at the edges, but they pull in different directions, and knowing where the line falls often decides whether you're protecting the next generation or leaving a mess behind.

Plain Facts About Estate Planning

Estate planning boils down to this: who handles your business if you can't, and who gets the house, the savings, or the headaches after you're gone. Most folks picture a will, and that's part of it, but it's only the start. The heart of it: putting paperwork in order so the right people have clear marching orders—while taxes, court fights, and the state stay on the sidelines as much as possible.

You'll see these pieces on almost any kitchen table meeting about estates:

- Will: Lays out where things go when you die. Names

who steps up for the kids if both parents are gone.

- Trust: Puts property under the care of someone who runs it by your rules. Could be revocable—meaning you can change your mind—or set up for a narrow purpose, like protecting a disabled child.
- Power of Attorney: Names a person who handles your money or health decisions if you're flat on your back or lose your faculties.
- Health Care Directive: What's to be done at the end. Life support, no life support, or naming the one who decides.
- Beneficiary Form: Used for life insurance or IRAs, sidestepping the whole probate process.

Done right, your plan covers more than death. It stands in for you if dementia hits, helps a business pass cleanly or lets you set down personal values in black and white. In practice, most families care less about skipping taxes and more about sparing the next generation court costs, conflict, or confusion.

What Medicaid Planning Actually Means

The word "Medicaid" gets thrown around once long-term care becomes real—not theoretical. Nursing home prices can run over $70,000 per year. Medicare won't touch most of it, which leaves Medicaid (MO HealthNet) holding the line for anyone who qualifies by medical and financial tests. The test is strict: the state wants you under $2,000 in countable assets if you're applying solo in 2024. Married couples face rules that get technical but aren't much looser.

Medicaid planning is less about who inherits, and more about not watching everything you've built vanish to a care bill. The game is in these moves:

Find ways to keep assets from being spent down to zero before you even qualify. Handle the five-year "look-back," where gifts or transfers get scrutinized and possibly penalized. Shape income and set up trusts so a healthy spouse or children hold onto something. Position yourself for eligibility—before it's too late—without losing the roof over your head.

You see irrevocable trusts show up here. Sometimes, folks buy certain annuities. Other times they turn "countable" cash into exempt property or time gifts with care. Done early, a chunk of what you earned might still end up with your family, and not in a ledger at the nursing facility.

Where They Part: Strategies, Goals, and Life Timing

Asset Transfer or Asset Defense?

Estate planning asks: who takes over when you don't, and how do you split things up after? Medicaid planning answers a much harder question: how do you keep from losing it all while you're still here? The two strategies overlap but point in different directions. Estate planning usually happens in advance at any age, but Medicaid planning turns urgent as retirement approaches, or health issues loom.

Different Tools, Different Consequences: Normal estate plans lean hard on wills, revocable trusts, and naming direct beneficiaries—to keep transfers smooth, taxes down, and lawyers out of your kitchen after death. Medicaid planning has little patience for that. It lives in the world of irrevocable trusts and "spend-down" maneuvers. For instance: a revocable trust may sidestep probate, but Medicaid still counts those assets. The kind of trust matters. Done wrong, someone thinking they're protected gets a rude awakening from the state.

The Real Divide: Lifetime Needs vs. After-Death Wishes

Estate plans mostly face forward—toward death, toward wishes carried out after you're gone. Medicaid planning cares what happens if you're still living, but require costly care that could burn through every resource. Protecting a spouse from eviction because of your medical bills is Medicaid work. Making sure your daughter gets the farm is classic estate planning.

How the Two Plans Interlock for Families

It's rare they stand alone. Estate and Medicaid planning run together like two streams in spring. If your estate plan ignores long-term care, your will may mean little after Medicaid fees eat up the savings. If you chase Medicaid eligibility with no attention to your big picture, you end up with assets strangled by restrictions or stuck in unusable structures. Pulling both threads matters.

It looks like this in real life:

A married pair gets wills and revocable trusts to keep things smooth. Then, as the years pass, a lawyer moves savings to an irrevocable trust. They wait out the five-year period before Medicaid sees those funds. Their kids, in the end, get something back.

A widow with savings fears winding up in a nursing home. Her attorney carves a plan that lets a trusted friend shift assets in an emergency—her power of attorney—plus a directive for health care choices. She adds a trigger in her documents that kicks in if Medicaid becomes necessary. This isn't fair weather work. It's built for the worst storm.

If long-term care never comes, the estate plan runs its course. If Medicaid is needed, the lifeboat's already built. It's not about outsmarting the state—it's about sheltering what matters when the test comes.

Moving Forward: Make the Plan Fit the Family

No single answer fits families. Each home has its own risks and priorities. What matters: building your shelter before the rain. When Medicaid and estate plans run side by side, security lasts longer and dignity survives the tough years. Find someone who knows the terrain. Honest planning, open eyes, and local experience will go further than guesswork or delay.

This isn't just about paperwork. It's peace, and the proof is in what's left standing after the storm.

ESTATE PLANNING WHEN LONG-TERM CARE IS ON THE HORIZON

Hard Realities: Long-Term Care Tied to Everything You've Worked For

Old age isn't what it used to be. People are living longer, but a long life means at some point, odds are that you'll need help with basic things—eating, getting dressed, even standing up in the morning. That help costs real money. Ask anyone who's priced a nursing home room. Upwards of seventy grand a year, and climbing, just to get steady hands when you need them most.

Families see what's coming. They worry about losing everything to care bills. People who spent decades earning, saving, building something for their children—suddenly they're told the only way to get care is to spend down to the last dollar. Most health insurance, even Medicare, will leave you hanging when it comes to long-term care. That's where Medicaid comes in. But qualifying for Medicaid means you have to fit through a narrow door. Without a plan, you risk leaving your family with nothing but memories.

Estate planning isn't just about passing down the family home after you die. It's about drawing your own line in the sand before the decisions get made for you. It's about control—of your savings, your home, your care, your legacy—when things get difficult.

The Tools That Matter Most—What Actually Protects You

Any decent estate plan takes long-term care into account. If you don't know who'll make your decisions when you can't, you leave the door open for a judge or the state. If you don't set up documents and trusts early enough, you shrink your own room to maneuver when the storm hits. Timing matters. So do the details.

Authority on Paper: Powers of Attorney and Directives

No one gets through this alone. You need people on your side, and you need to put their names in writing. A Durable Power of Attorney for Financial Decisions lets your trusted person—maybe a child, a spouse, someone with their feet on the ground—pay bills, handle accounts, deal with red tape, all without waiting for a judge to say so. That's the difference between keeping the lights on or letting the bank come calling.

You also want aDurable Power of Attorney for Health Care—someone who can talk to doctors, sign the paperwork, and decide if the hospital or the nursing home is the right call.
Advance Health Care Directive makes clear what you want if things get bad. You lift a heavy burden off your family's shoulders by spelling out how far to go with medical care.

Wills and Trusts—Traditional, but Still the Backbone

A Last Will and Testament is the starting place for dividing up what's left after you're gone. It does nothing to protect assets while you're alive or facing nursing home bills. For that, you look to trusts.

Revocable Living Trusts help you during your lifetime—if you get sick or lose capacity, your backup trustee steps in. You stay out of probate court. But Medicaid isn't fooled. If the trust is revocable, your money is still on the table for care costs.

For seniors who plan ahead, irrevocable trusts can shelter specific assets—usually a home or savings—so Medicaid won't count them. Here's the catch: you have to do it early, at least five years before you need Medicaid. That "look-back" rule is strict. Don't count on last-minute fixes.

If you go that route, the trust has to be airtight under the law and Medicaid rules. Assets in the trust are out of your reach, so don't lock away what you still need to live. But when done right, an irrevocable trust can protect your life's work for your family's future, not the nursing home.

Other Ways to Guard What You Built—But Tread Lightly

There's the state Homestead Exemption. It can keep a chunk of your home's value out of probate and, sometimes, out of Medicaid's grasp. But the numbers are small, and most people's homes far exceed the cap. It's a tool, not a shield.

Some folks try handing over property or cash to their children—gifting it away to hide it from Medicaid. That move backfires more than people realize. Give something away within five years of applying for Medicaid and you face a penalty period. Your eligibility gets delayed, and your kids' problems with creditors, divorce, or bankruptcy just became your problems too.

Long-term care insurance gets tossed around, but by the time the need is clear, it's often too expensive or just not available for those in shaky health. The window closes fast.

The Gritty Details—Medicaid Rules

MO HealthNet (Missouri's Medicaid) holds the keys to most long-term care help. But the rules are tight. In 2024, a single person can't have more than $5,726 in countable resources. You can keep a house (up to a certain equity value), one car, and personal items. Most of the rest—bank accounts, other property—counts against you. Other states have similar rules and you need to verify – either with a license attorney or your state Medicaid office.

Income limits add another layer. If income runs too high for Medicaid, you may be able to use a Qualified Income Trust (QIT), sometimes called a Miller Trust. It routes the extra income the right way, keeping you in the running for help when care costs could steamroll you.

Married couples get one break: the Community Spouse Resource Allowance. The healthy spouse at home can keep a set amount of assets and income. Planning carefully here can make sure the spouse left at home isn't left out in the cold.

And after death, Medicaid wants payback. Estate recovery means the state makes claims to recoup what it spent on your care. Good estate planning can blunt that. The legacy you intended for family doesn't have to vanish the day you die.

When to Act—And What Happens If You're Running Out of Time

Power belongs to those who plan before the waters rise. Start talking and gathering facts in your early sixties—don't wait for a diagnosis or a hospital trip to get serious. Even those coming up on a crisis have options, but the choices grow thin as time slips away.

Step one: round up your essentials. Deeds. Bank statements. Retirement and insurance policies. Old wills. Updated beneficiaries. Put them together in a place your trusted people can find. Know how much long-term care really costs. Talk through what you want and who you trust. Reality—not wishful thinking—ought to shape every decision.

A lawyer who knows this field is worth every penny. Regulations change, forms matter, and each family's situation has cracks where something can fall through. Work with someone who will listen, then draft a plan that fits not just the law, but your hopes for the people you leave behind.

The Bottom Line

Getting old is a battle against losing control. If you prepare, the rules work in your favor. Miss the window, and the system decides for you—about your savings, your care, your family's future. Powers of attorney, advance directives, wills, and the right trusts build your defenses. Know the Medicaid rules. Put things in order while you still can. That's how you keep hold of what you spent your life building.

Don't gamble with your legacy. Whatever stage you're at—map it out with someone who's been through this drill before. It's the difference between leaving a burden and leaving a blessing.

SECTION 6: PROBATE & ASSET TRANSFER

PROBATE COURT: WHAT YOU NEED TO KNOW

Probate Court oversees the legal process of validating a deceased person's will, identifying and inventorying their assets, paying debts and taxes, and distributing remaining property to heirs or beneficiaries. This court-supervised process ensures a decedent's estate is settled according to law.

Nobody wants to deal with court when they're grieving. That's the hard truth about probate. It's a legal process that many people misunderstand, often seeing it as an automatic headache. Sometimes it is. Other times, it's a necessary step to ensure an estate is handled properly.

Understanding the Probate Court system is crucial for anyone planning their estate or dealing with the loss of a loved one. It dictates how assets are transferred, debts are paid, and legacies are honored. Let's break it down.

What Exactly is Probate Court?

At its core, probate is the legal process that proves a will is valid (if one exists), identifies the deceased person's property, pays their debts and taxes, and distributes what's left to the rightful heirs or beneficiaries. It's a court-supervised process. That's the key.

When someone passes away, their assets don't just magically transfer. If those assets are solely in their name, without a co-owner or a designated beneficiary, they typically have to go through probate. This includes things like real estate, bank accounts, investments, and personal property.

The probate court in each county handles these matters. Their job is to make sure everything is done by the book. This protects creditors, ensures taxes are paid, and ultimately, that the wishes of the deceased are carried out, or that state law is followed if there's no will.

The Probate Process: A Step-by-Step Breakdown

The probate process isn't a quick trip to the courthouse. It involves several distinct phases. Knowing these steps helps manage expectations and navigate the system.

1. Opening the Estate

This is where it all begins. Someone—usually a family member or the executor named in the will—files a petition with the Probate Court. They ask the court to officially appoint a personal representative. If there's a will, the court will validate it and issue "letters testamentary" to the executor. If there's no will, the court issues "letters of administration" and appoints an administrator, following state laws of intestacy. This person is now legally responsible for managing the estate.

2. Notifying Creditors

Once the personal representative is appointed, they have to notify all known creditors of the deceased. They also publish a general notice in a local newspaper. Creditors then have a specific timeframe, usually six months from the date of publication, to file claims against the estate. This step is critical for settling debts before assets are distributed.

3. Inventory and Appraisal

The personal representative must identify and list all of the deceased's assets. This includes everything from real estate and bank accounts to cars, jewelry, and household items. Sometimes, professional appraisals are needed to determine the value of certain assets. This inventory is filed with the court.

4. Paying Debts and Taxes

Legitimate creditor claims approved by the court, along with any final income taxes, estate taxes (rare for most estates), and administrative expenses (like attorney fees and court costs), must be paid from the estate's funds. The law dictates the priority of these payments.

5. Distribution of Assets

After all debts, taxes, and expenses are paid, the remaining assets are distributed. If there's a will, assets go to the named beneficiaries. If there's no will, intestacy laws determine who inherits what. This usually means spouses, children, or other close relatives. Once everything is distributed, the personal representative files a final accounting with the court.

6. Closing the Estate

The final step is to formally close the estate. The personal representative petitions the court for discharge, signifying that all duties have been fulfilled. The court then issues an order closing the estate, and the personal representative is relieved of their responsibilities.

Why You Might Want to Avoid Probate

Probate is a public process. This means details about the deceased's assets, debts, and who inherits what become public record. For many families, this lack of privacy is a significant concern.

It's also often time-consuming. A typical probate can take anywhere from six months to a year, or even longer for complex estates or those with disputes. This delay can be frustrating for beneficiaries waiting for their inheritance.

And then there's the cost. Attorney fees, court costs, appraisal fees, publication fees, and personal representative commissions can quickly add up. These expenses reduce the amount of inheritance passed on to your loved ones.

Strategies for Avoiding Probate

The good news is that with careful planning, many assets can bypass Probate Court entirely. This is a core component of effective estate planning.

HOW LONG PROBATE REALLY TAKES

Step-By-Step: Parsing the Probate Process

Probate isn't math; it's more like clearing a field after a storm. Someone passes, and suddenly you're sorting their will—if they even had one—and someone has to step up as personal representative. Now you're hunting down assets, handling old debts, and parceling out what's left to the people named or next in line. The big question most folks have: how long until it's finished?

No one has a stopwatch for probate. Some estates move quick—most don't. The timeline hinges on the estate's size, how tangled things are, what type of court procedure applies, and plain luck: whether relatives get along, and if you can handle the mountain of paperwork without dropping something important. Six months to a year is normal. That's the middle of the road. Where you have a messy estate—with property, angry heirs, taxes, and lost paperwork—it can drag out years.

Getting Started: Filing and Appointment

Probate starts plain enough. Somebody brings a will, if it exists, and a probate petition down to the courthouse in the county where the person lived. The state says you have as certain amount of time from the death to file the will. Most people don't wait that long, but sometimes families freeze up in the headlights. After the paperwork lands on the clerk's desk, you wait for a hearing so the court can tap someone as personal representative—either executor (named in a will) or administrator (if there's no will). A hearing could pop up in a month. Or you wait. Sometimes several months pass, just for that first court date.

Once the personal representative is official, the court gives them "letters"—either testamentary or of administration. Now, the heavy lifting starts: collecting account balances, securing property, alerting the right people. Nothing is fast. Every step needs proof.

Notifying Creditors and Waiting Out the Clock

Under the law, you must reach out to every known creditor as soon as probate kicks off. That's only half the job. You're also required to publish a public notice to unknown creditors, once a week, two weeks running, in a local paper. This isn't just paperwork—it triggers a waiting period. Creditors now have six months from the first publication to file their claims. That's the floor. Nothing wraps before then. Even if you're otherwise ready to close, the estate stays open, waiting for stray claims.

In practice, estates remain open well past six months. Sorting claims, investigating debts, selling property if you have to—it all takes time. And the court won't close up shop until every reason for someone to object is gone.

Inventory, Appraisal, and Settling Debts

The personal representative has thirty days from appointment to file a list of assets with the court. That's everything: houses, vehicles, accounts, investments, even things like farm tools or a gun safe. For a simple estate, this looks like a spreadsheet. For anything big or strange, you might need real appraisers or help from financial pros, and waiting on them can stretch the process further.

Debts have to be sorted and paid. Taxes as well. Sometimes you have to sell family land or grandma's antiques to make things balance out between heirs—or to pay the IRS. Disagreements over what things are worth, or even who gets what, will always add months onto the clock. Sometimes, it's years.

Final Accounting and Closing the Doors

At the end, the personal representative files a final accounting. This document recaps every dollar in, every dollar out, and lays out what each beneficiary should get. Beneficiaries can review and dispute it if something looks off. If the court signs off, the last assets get handed over and someone files to close the probate.

If it all sails through clean, an estate with little drama wraps in about eight to twelve months. If you hit snags—property fights, tax questions, missing paperwork, or angry family members—plan for delays. The court's own backlog can slow things down, too. Simple never means easy.

What Can Drag Out Probate?

Several sticking points show up again and again in probate. Here's what slows the works:

- Large or Complex Estates:
  The more assets or business interests, the more forms, the more human error. Everything takes longer when you have to track down paperwork or chase banks across state lines.
- Independent or Supervised Probate:
  "Independent" means fewer court check-ins—faster, if family agrees. "Supervised" gives the court control and can drag things out with extra hearings.
- Fighting Among Heirs or Creditors:
  Any dispute—over a will, a debt, or who should inherit—stops the clock. Some fights never get resolved without hearings, even trials. That adds serious time.
- Lots of Creditor Claims:
  If the deceased left behind debt, it can take a long

while to sell assets, reach deals, and cut checks before anything goes to heirs.

- Real Estate, Especially Out-of-State:
  Land in another state can require juggling multiple court systems. Every mile away from your state brings another pile of forms.
- Tax Complications:
  Owing federal estate tax or sorting old returns means more delay. The IRS works on their schedule, not yours.
- Court Delays: Some counties are overloaded. The pile of cases in a particular courthouse may push yours to the back of the line, sometimes for months at a time.

A Word About Administration Style

"Independent administration" gives the personal representative freedom: fewer mandatory court touchpoints, fewer delays, as long as every heir is on board. "Supervised administration" means the court watches each step—meetings, deadlines, every sale or transfer. Independent cases generally close sooner, unless a problem erupts. If the will doesn't require supervision or if heirs agree, push for independence to keep things moving. Cooperation makes all the difference.

How to Keep Probate From Dragging On

You can't erase the creditor waiting period, but you don't have to invite more delay. Here's what tends to move probate along:

File Right Away:
Don't wait months to file the will or open probate. The longer you delay, the longer the case takes.

Get Your Paperwork Together:
Being organized matters. A clean list of assets, debts, and heirs keeps everyone honest and speeds up every part of the process.

Stay in Touch:
Let heirs know what's happening. Silence breeds suspicion, and fights cause delays.

Review If the Estate Qualifies as a Small Estate:
If the numbers work, use the shortcut.

Bring in a Pro:
An experienced probate attorney plugs holes and keeps the process from freezing over a technicality.

HOW TO STEER CLEAR OF PROBATE: DIRECT MOVES TO SAFEGUARD WHAT YOU'VE BUILT

Look Probate in the Eye—and Understand Why People Dodge It

After someone dies, the clock starts. Probate kicks in—a court-run track that inventories your valuables, pays what you owe, sorts through taxes, and then parcels out the rest to whoever is next in line. The whole thing can drag on for months. Lawyers may need paying. So do clerks. The process is slow, costs add up, and every detail goes public. Anyone curious enough can dig through records and see which way your money and property went.

Plenty of folks here want none of it. They'd rather save their families time and trouble, cut down on legal expenses, and keep family business private. Probate weighs on survivors. Avoiding it makes for a lighter load after you're gone, and gets your wishes handled without delay.

Revocable Living Trusts—The Workhorse

We have talked about them at length already. Here's the deal. You need one. Talk to an attorney.

Transfer on Death

A Transfer On Death (TOD) Deed is a legal document that allows a property owner to name a beneficiary who will automatically receive their real estate upon the owner's death, bypassing the probate court process. This deed must be properly executed and recorded during the owner's lifetime to be effective.

What is a Transfer On Death Deed, Anyway?

Let's talk real estate. You own a home, a farm, or some land. When you die, that property usually goes through probate. It's a court process. It can be slow. It can cost money. A lot of people want to avoid that.

That's where the Transfer On Death Deed comes in. It's a simple tool. You sign a deed today, naming a beneficiary. That beneficiary gets the property when you die. No probate. It happens automatically. You keep full control of your property while you're alive. You can sell it, mortgage it, or even revoke the TODD anytime you want. The deed only "kicks in" when you're gone.

How Does a TODD Work?

The process for creating a Transfer On Death Deed is pretty direct, but you need to get it right. First, you draft the deed. This document must clearly identify the property, the owner (you, the grantor), and the person or people who will receive the property (the beneficiary or beneficiaries).

Once drafted, you sign it. This isn't a casual signature. It needs to be notarized. This step proves you're the one signing and that you're doing so intentionally. After it's signed and notarized, the crucial final step is recording. You must record the deed with the Recorder of Deeds in the county where the property is located. This has to happen during your lifetime. If it's not recorded, it's not valid.

You retain full ownership and control. You can sell the property. You can put a mortgage on it. You can even change your mind and revoke the TODD. You do this by recording a new deed or a specific revocation document. The beneficiary has no rights to the property until you pass away. It's a powerful feature, offering flexibility while providing a clear path for transfer.

A TODD is a simple tool for a specific job: transferring real property. If you own your home outright or have a clear plan for who should inherit it, a TODD can be a very effective part of your overall estate planning strategy. It's not a full estate plan on its own, but it handles one big piece of the puzzle efficiently.

Key Considerations and Potential Pitfalls

While a Transfer On Death Deed offers clear advantages, it's not a one-size-fits-all solution. There are critical points to consider.

Beneficiary Issues

What if your named beneficiary dies before you do? The deed should specify what happens then. Does it go to their children (per stirpes)? Does it go to your other named beneficiaries? If not specified, the property might revert to your estate, potentially pushing it back into probate. Clear beneficiary designations are paramount.

Estate Planning Integration

A TODD is a single arrow in your quiver. It's not the whole arsenal. It needs to work in harmony with your will, trusts, and powers of attorney. A poorly integrated TODD could contradict other parts of your plan, creating confusion and conflict for your heirs. For instance, if your will states your property goes to your church, but your TODD names your nephew, the TODD generally wins for that specific property.

Is a Transfer On Death Deed Right for Your Property?

This isn't a rhetorical question. If you have a relatively simple estate, a clear idea of who should get your home, and you want to avoid probate, it's worth considering. It's especially useful for single individuals or married couples with adult children who simply want to pass their primary residence directly.

However, if your situation is more complex—say, you have minor children, special needs beneficiaries, multiple properties, significant debts, or you're concerned about Medicaid recovery—a TODD alone might not cut it. You might need a trust, a more detailed will, or other estate planning tools to achieve your goals effectively.

The key here is "fit." Does this tool fit your specific needs and goals? Does it align with your broader financial and legacy plans? Without a clear understanding of your individual circumstances, it's impossible to say for sure.

Don't Go It Alone: Get Professional Advice

The rules around real estate and estate planning are detailed. The law, like all state laws, has its nuances. Trying to navigate this without experienced guidance can lead to mistakes that cost your family time, money, and stress down the road. A simple oversight in drafting or recording a Transfer On Death Deed can render it useless.

An estate planning attorney can help you determine if a TODD is the right choice for you. They can ensure it's correctly drafted, executed, and recorded. More importantly, they can help you integrate it into a comprehensive estate plan that addresses all your assets, liabilities, and wishes. Don't leave your family's future to chance.

The Transfer On Death Deed is a valuable tool for transferring real estate outside of probate. It offers simplicity, cost savings, and efficiency. But like any legal instrument, it comes with specific requirements and potential complexities. Understanding how it interacts with other aspects of your estate, such as beneficiary designations, Medicaid, and creditor claims, is essential. For property owners it can be a cornerstone of a well-thought-out estate plan. Just make sure you get it right the first time.

SECTION 7: SPECIAL TOPICS

WHY YOU PLAN ASSET PROTECTION BEFORE TROUBLE FINDS YOU

Ground Rules for Protecting What's Yours

When a sheriff's car rolls up or a certified letter lands on your porch, it's already too late. Asset protection isn't a luxury; it's a shield made of timing and foresight. The reasons to worry are plenty: lawsuits pile up at the door, creditors hunt, marriages break, medical bills explode, economies collapse. That's the terrain. The law gives you the tools—a mix of old methods and new paperwork—but only if you grip them before disaster knocks. Lay the groundwork when the sun's still out. Wait for the clouds, and your grip won't matter.

Everything you build—retirement, the house you raised kids in, a family stake in a business—can go up for grabs once a claim surfaces. The law lays out your options. You can retitle property, lean on exemptions, form an LLC, or trust an ironclad trust. But every option has an invisible tripwire. The law remembers when you act. If you make your move after a threat appears, courts will see through it. You may even dig yourself in deeper. The law isn't fooled by frantic switches or hasty signatures.

Most people picture asset protection as big legal maneuvers, but sometimes it's as simple as holding property with a spouse—homestead exemption keeps a small shield on your primary home. LLCs split business risk from your personal savings. Irrevocable trusts—done right, at the right time—can move assets out of easy reach. These shields only work if you forge them before any shadow crosses your horizon. Scramble when a lawsuit's filed, and you only add suspicion. Courts don't just ignore those late plays; they might call them fraud.

Why Timing Decides Everything

The law has a long memory and no patience for last-minute transfers. If a storm is already brewing, or the lawsuit's already hung over your head, and you shuffle your assets, the law isn't on your side. Those acts—the quick property giveaway, the hasty trust—are called fraudulent transfers. If a judge suspects you're just trying to duck creditors, they'll snap the assets back. Worse, they'll add new penalties.

This isn't just on paper. Courts use these rules. Sell the farm to a cousin the day after a demand letter arrives? Transfer investments to your son's name while you're under legal threat? That paperwork won't hold. Even if you mean well or feel cornered, those moves look suspicious once legal trouble is real. Malpractice, old debts, injuries from a workplace accident—these can all bring your timing under review.

If you plan years ahead, the record shows your purpose is clean: keeping business squared away, securing family plans, maybe old-school estate planning. Judges rarely challenge assets tucked away and left untouched for years. Early planning delivers more than a legal edge—you get to sleep at night, instead of waiting for a process server out front.

When Last-Minute Desperation Turns Costly

Take Anne—she runs a small business, looks after her savings, thinks about retirement but expects tomorrow to look much like today. Then she's sued out of nowhere by an angry former client. Panic sets in. Anne shuttles her investments to her kids. She moves her properties into a fresh trust. She's moving fast, hoping the new paperwork forms a wall. The court can unwind the whole maneuver. Anne's savings lie exposed again, and now there's a whisper of fraud behind her name.

If Anne had sorted her business inside an LLC early, put an asset protection trust in place, and kept her business and personal money cleanly divided, that storm wouldn't have collapsed her walls. Pre-crisis structure stands up in court. Last-minute panic is a dead giveaway.

Tried-and-True Protection Tools

The tools are familiar, but they work only if you have patience and discipline:

Homestead exemption:
Up to $15,000 of your main home's equity is shielded from most creditors. Not much for expensive homes, but it's something. If you want to save more than that, you'll need another layer.

Tenancy by the entirety:
Married partners can own real estate as one unit. Creditors chasing one spouse usually can't touch that home. It's old-fashioned, but reliable in the right case.

LLCs—Limited Liability Companies:
Put your rentals or shop in an LLC, and you've built a wall between your business risks and your home savings. Courts honor that wall, as long as your business paperwork is clean and you don't mix personal with business cash.

Irrevocable trusts:
Done early, these move assets out of your legal reach, blocking future creditors. A revocable trust can be changed. An irrevocable one can't. Only the latter counts as real asset protection against a determined creditor.

Spendthrift provisions:

Write these into your trust, and heirs can't lose everything to divorce, gambling, or bad debt. Useful when family lines are complicated or tempers run hot.

Retirement accounts:
State law and federal law protect many IRAs and similar accounts. But only if you set them up right. Details matter. A mistake here can waste the shield entirely.

Every one of these breaks down if you wait until the wolves are on the porch. Judges read the calendar. If your changes show up late, you lose the benefit and draw suspicion. Hire local legal help before you need it. That's the only way to keep the roof up when the storm hits.

The Stories People Get Wrong

Many think asset protection is about hiding money. It's not. The law doesn't reward the dishonest, and courts dig deep if something smells off. These tools let you arrange your property for the long haul—protecting your family, supporting retirement, even aiding a charity once you're gone. Risk never leaves life, but preparation lets you keep hold of what you've built.

The next myth says only the wealthy or doctors need to worry. That's fantasy. Anyone with a home, a little savings, a shop on Main Street, or a side business is a target. Lawsuits aren't picky. Divorce, injury, or a bad financial turn hit all sorts.

The last myth says an asset protection plan is set in wet concrete. Not true. Certain moves—like irrevocable trusts—are stiff by design. But for most tools, you can adapt as life changes. What never changes is this: you have to act before the trouble starts. Storm prep saves houses, not sandbags stacked in the rain.

If You Wait, You Pay

Don't mistake calm for safety. Wait too long, and your careful savings, your house, your business—all of it—can be stripped by one bad lawsuit, a tough divorce, or an illness that drains your cash. Once someone comes for your assets, your toolkit gets very small, very fast. Almost nothing stands up against creditors if you try to build your defenses after the attack starts.

The last-second fixes don't work. Sign over a deed or shift cash as the crisis bites, and courts will see through it. They may call it fraud. In some cases, you'll lose more than you protect. You may even look less trustworthy in front of a judge or jury. Do it ahead of time, and you have options tailored to you—controlled on your timeline.

Asset protection has to sync with estate plans, tax law, and all the quirks of paperwork. A mistake with titles or trust language creates hassle and expense for your family. You want your legacy to move without confusion. A good lawyer keeps the handoff smooth and sharp.

Work with a Attorney—Before You Need One

This isn't a job for the internet or a fill-in-the-blank form. State rules are complex, and every situation is a one-off puzzle. A lawyer who knows their ground will keep you within the rules, lay out all your options, and make sure your family actually sees the results after you're gone.

An attorney maps out your assets, the risks you face now, and what might come later. The earlier you get started—while trouble is out of sight—the fewer obstacles or surprises when you need the plan to hold.

If you act now, you move with strength, not fear. Waiting guarantees only that you'll be running behind. Prevention always trumps panic. Build the wall before you see the first enemy on the horizon.

FINAL THOUGHT

Eighteen hits hard, whether you're ready or not. The law says their grown. The birthday cards pile up and high school fades. Young adults across the country step out, call their own shots, sometimes without looking back. But behind the scenes, another change clicks into place. Medical info—that web of doctors, charts, emergencies—shuts tight. Parents suddenly hit a wall, regardless of how many insurance premiums they pay. When it gets serious, a HIPAA Authorization holds the keys. Without it, even the best intentions don't open a single hospital door.

HIPAA at Eighteen: Rights End, Rules Tighten

We've talked about that at length, but older adults need to think about this too. Just recently, I was misbilled by a doctor's office in town. They sent me a bill for services I paid for. I sent my wife to get a copy of the invoices while I was at work. They turned her down flat. She had to come to my office and pick up a HIPAA authorization. Everyone needs one - not just the kids.

GLOSSARY

Administrator: A person appointed by the court to manage an estate when there is no will or no executor named.

Beneficiary: A person or entity designated to receive assets from a trust, will, life insurance policy, or retirement account.

Codicil: A legal document that modifies, adds to, or revokes provisions in an existing will.

Conservator: A person appointed by the court to manage the financial affairs of someone unable to do so themselves.

Durable Power of Attorney: A legal document authorizing someone to make financial decisions on your behalf, remaining valid even if you become incapacitated.

Estate: All the assets and liabilities a person owns at death, including real estate, bank accounts, investments, and personal property.

Estate Tax: A federal tax imposed on the transfer of property at death (currently only applies to estates over $13.61 million in 2024).

Executor: The person named in a will to carry out its instructions and manage the estate through probate.

Fiduciary: A person in a position of trust who must act in the best interests of another, such as an executor, trustee, or agent under a power of attorney.

Grantor: The person who creates a trust and transfers assets into it (also called settlor or trustor).

Guardian: A person appointed to care for a minor child or incapacitated adult.

Health Care Power of Attorney: A document naming someone to make medical decisions on your behalf if you cannot.

HIPAA Authorization: A document allowing designated people to access your protected health information.

Incapacitated: Unable to make or communicate informed decisions about personal or financial matters.

Intestate: Dying without a valid will, causing state law to determine how assets are distributed.

Irrevocable Trust: A trust that cannot be modified or terminated without the beneficiary's permission.

Joint Tenancy with Right of Survivorship: Property ownership where the surviving owner automatically inherits the deceased owner's share.

Living Will: A document stating your wishes for end-of-life medical treatment (different from a living trust).

Medicaid: A joint federal-state program providing health coverage for individuals with limited income and assets, including long-term care.

Per Stirpes: A method of distributing assets where a deceased beneficiary's share passes to their descendants.

Personal Representative: Another term for executor or administrator.

Probate: The court-supervised process of validating a will, paying debts, and distributing assets.

Revocable Living Trust: A trust that can be modified or terminated during the grantor's lifetime and avoids probate at death.

Special Needs Trust: A trust designed to provide for a disabled beneficiary without disqualifying them from government benefits.

Successor Trustee: The person or entity designated to manage a trust after the original trustee dies, resigns, or becomes incapacitated.

Tenancy by the Entirety: A form of joint ownership between spouses where both must agree to sell or transfer the property.

Testator: A person who makes a will.

Transfer on Death (TOD) Deed: A deed that automatically transfers real estate to named beneficiaries at death, avoiding probate.

Trust: A legal arrangement where one person (the trustee) holds and manages property for the benefit of another (the beneficiary).

Trustee: The person or institution responsible for managing trust assets according to the trust's terms.

Will: A legal document stating how you want your assets distributed after death and naming guardians for minor children.

CONCLUSION: WHAT HAPPENS NEXT

You've made it through seven sections on wills, trusts, guardianship, Medicaid, probate, and every other topic that makes most people's eyes glaze over. That means something.

It means you care enough about the people who depend on you to do the work most folks avoid.

So what happens next?

If you're in Missouri, call my office. We'll sit down, go through your specific situation, and build a plan that actually fits your life. No cookie-cutter templates, no paralegal assembly line. Just straightforward planning that covers what you own and who you love.

If you're outside Missouri, take what you've learned here and find an attorney in your state who thinks like this—someone who explains things in plain English, who doesn't hide behind legal jargon, and who builds plans meant to work in the real world, not just look impressive in a binder.

Either way, don't let this book collect dust.

The information in here only helps if you act on it.

Estate planning isn't about death. It's about taking care of the people you'd protect if you were still here. It's one of the few ways we get to keep looking after our families even when we can't be there ourselves.

That's worth doing right.

— Patrick Nolan

ABOUT THE AUTHOR

Patrick Nolan is an estate planning attorney and founder of Nolan Law Firm in Missouri. A combat veteran and former reporter, he brings a systematic, no-nonsense approach to helping families protect what they've built.

Patrick specializes in preventative law—the work you do before problems arrive—and has built a practice around flat-fee estate planning rather than billable hours. His approach combines military discipline, journalistic clarity, and a deep skepticism of overcomplicated solutions that lawyers love but clients can't use.

He's the author of "The Unfinished Republic" and "Small Claims Court Handbook," and publishes ongoing legal education through PatTalksLaw and Practical Legal Tech.

Patrick lives in Missouri with his family and remains committed to the importance of proper planning.

Contact Information:
Nolan Law Firm
Phone: 660.956.4502
Website: nemolegal.com

Made in United States
North Haven, CT
06 November 2026

21875927R00085